"Informing the world about Islam's place in America, this book could not come at a more opportune moment. Lucid, erudite and provocative, only Amir Hussain can make us see the multiple dimensions of the world's second largest faith in America's cultural icons, musical stars, political history, cultural values, and public life at large in his unique masterful style. A must-read for anyone wishing to observe Islam beyond sensational headlines in order to grasp the complex lives of Muslim Americans."

—EBRAHIM MOOSA, *Professor of Islamic Studies and Religion, University of Notre Dame*

"Muslims and the Making of America is an accessible and engaging book that tells the story of Muslim contributions to American history and creativity. From early medieval intimations of an 'unknown land' across the Atlantic, through west African plantation slaves, to the contemporary accomplishments of athletes, musicians, and artists, Islam has been a force in the United States and Muslims have played a vital role in making America great."

—JANE MCAULIFFE, *Director of National and International Outreach, United States Library of Congress*

"A sparkling text. Amir Hussain arrives early to tell a story that has long needed telling."

—JACK MILES, *Distinguished Professor of English and Religious Studies, University of California at Irvine*

Muslims and the Making of America

Amir Hussain

BAYLOR UNIVERSITY PRESS

Cover design by Will Brown
Cover photograph: Pakistani-American Muslim DJ "Ms. DiJa"
at the Inner-City Muslim Action Network (IMAN) in Chicago,
Illinois. © 2007 Kauthar Umar, isl • am • erica.

This book has been cataloged by the Library of Congress.

Printed in the United States of America on acid-free paper with
a minimum of 30 percent post-consumer waste recycled content.

*I am the most fortunate of people because my first and
greatest teachers, my parents, are still alive and with me.
This book is dedicated to them.*

—For Feroza and Iqbal Hussain—

"Your Lord has decreed that you worship none but God,
and show goodness to your parents. If one or both of
them reach old age with you, say not to them a word of
disrespect but speak to them a gracious word. And lower
unto them the wing of humility through mercy, and say:
'My Lord! Have mercy on them both as they did care for
me when I was little.'"

—Qur'an 17:23-24

*My parents and their generation were not the pioneers
of Islam in Canada, but for the past fifty years
they have helped in the development of Canadian Muslim
communities. Here in the United States,
the two American Muslims who I think most influenced
American culture, and who certainly had the most influence
on me, were Ahmet Ertegun (1923–2006) and
Muhammad Ali (1942–2016).
May God be pleased with them both.
They were both exemplars of American Muslims who in
the words of our grandmother, the blessed Maya Angelou,
helped us to "be and be better."
Our country is the richer for their contributions,
and so this book is also dedicated to them.*

Contents

Acknowledgments

Quite simply, this book would not have been possible without the work of one man, Carey C. Newman, the Director of Baylor University Press. Carey came to me with the idea for this book so many years ago that I'm embarrassed to write down the date. He suffered patiently while I developed my ideas for this book and worked on other projects. If he thought there were days that this book might not actually get finished, he had the graciousness not to share those reservations with me. The staff at Baylor University Press also deserve thanks for their help in making this book a reality. In particular, I'd like to thank Cade Jarrell, Stephanie Hoffman, and Grace Wallace for manuscript preparation and image research; Jenny Hunt for copyediting; Diane Smith for layout and design; and David Aycock for marketing and promotion work.

This book is the richer for having been developed while I taught a first-year seminar for each of the past three years at Loyola Marymount University on Islam and the Building of America. I thank my students for helping me to think through the ideas presented in this book in those classes. I especially thank Katherine Merkl, who was a student in one of those classes and then became my Rains research assistant for this book, helping me to do much of the preliminary historical research. I am also thankful to the Los Angeles Institute for the Humanities for allowing me to present this as a work in progress, and get feedback to help make this a much better book.

I am indebted to the work of countless colleagues in the study of Islam who have been the pilgrims in the academic work on Islam in America, and who have shared their wisdom with me. I will not mention any of them by name here, as I will inevitably forget someone. But in reading these pages, whether explicitly mentioned in them or not, you know who you are, and you know the debt of gratitude that I owe to you. Thank you.

Introduction
The American Ideal and Islam

"In heart I am a Moslem; in heart I am an American"

—a line in Patti Smith's "Babelogue," 1978

BEGINNINGS

There has never been an America without Muslims. Let that sink in for those who think that Muslims are relative newcomers to this county. We were here long before 1776, brought over first as slaves from West Africa. We weren't large in number in those colonial days, but that number has grown to about seven million of us here now in these United States. Over those centuries (and I emphasize, *centuries*), we have woven ourselves into the fabric that is American life. However, you wouldn't know that from comments that paint Islam as an "un-American" religion, with some even seeking to ban all Muslims from our shores. These prejudiced statements have popularity because most of us don't know a Muslim. In 2014 one of the Pew Forum polls revealed that only 38 percent of Americans know a Muslim. To put that in the negative, over 60 percent of Americans say they don't know a Muslim. Perhaps they do, but just don't know it. Perhaps it's no different than, say, with LGBTQ Americans, where one often has to add the qualifier "that they know of," meaning people may not know someone who is openly LGBTQ, just like they may not know someone who is "openly" Muslim. But think for a moment. All of us know at least one American Muslim, the Greatest of All Time.

Perhaps the most famous person (not just the most famous athlete, but the most famous human being) in the world was an American Muslim, Muhammad Ali. And his was a fame that was earned before the Internet or the World Wide Web or social media. Of him, my friend Gary Smith wrote the following in the cover story "A Celebration of Muhammad Ali" for *Sports Illustrated* on November 15, 1989 (that Ali has appeared more than anyone else on the cover of *Sports Illustrated* is but one measure of his fame), about the changes in Ali's life due to Parkinson's syndrome:

> What was this but metamorphosis? What was this but another face of that which made Muhammad Ali the most dominant figure in sports of the past 35 years, of any 35 years, of all time. All of his life was transformation: Ali's soul knew the butterfly's secret as well as his feet knew its dance. From Cassius Clay to Muhammad Ali, from Christian to Muslim. From the man who told the government where to stick its draft to the one who endorsed Ronald Reagan. From the boxer women loved, the dancer who whirled and flitted so his pretty face was never touched—to the boxer men loved, who stood and took the thunder from the thunder throwers, from the Foremans and the Fraziers. From the king of the world—to the man on his knees with his forehead pressed to the prayer rug. From madman to poet to circus barker to preacher to clown to magician to . . .

Before the big fights these days, when he is introduced in the ring, I see all the pity and pain on people's faces when he gives that little wave, that glazed look across the audience, and makes that exit through the ring ropes that seems to last forever. I see all the people who wanted him to be a symbol of something wonderful and liberating for all of his life, for all of their lives.

Look once more, look harder, I want to nudge them and say.

He is.

We go into greater detail about Ali's life in the third chapter of this book, but think about him for a minute if you think you don't know an American Muslim. Think about his life and legacy. Think of the media coverage around the world and the outpouring of support and goodwill following his death on June 3, 2016. Ali has been one of my own heroes for almost as long as I can remember. I was eight when he fought George Foreman in Zaire, the fight that came to be known in those less enlightened days as "The Rumble in the Jungle." I wasn't afraid that Ali would merely *lose*; I was worried that he would *die* at the hands of Foreman. Today, George Foreman is jolly, old, and fat, a lovable late night TV pitchman. However, in 1974 he wasn't the second coming of Santa Claus, but the Baddest Man in America. In those days, George Foreman, I write with all due respect, was thought to be a Thug. He had emerged from the Fifth Ward of Houston, the worst place in America at that time to be a young man. Coming out of the toughest ghetto in America, he was the most famous puncher of his day (with all due respect to Ken Norton and Joe Frazier), and no one in his right mind wanted to be hit by him.

So what did Muhammad Ali do? As usual, he defied conventional wisdom, and "took the thunder from the thunder throwers." He let Foreman hit him. He let Foreman hit him with those murderous blows, slipping many of them with his quickness and deflecting others with his skill. In the clinches in between, he whispered into Foreman's ear. "Is that all you got? Is that all you got, George?" It *was* all Foreman had, and with that "Rope a Dope" technique, Ali was able to tire out Foreman, and knock him out in the eighth round to win the fight. And Ali did this on the continent of Africa, not in America, adding to his legend around the world.

If we thought about Ali in the days before his death, what probably came to mind was the image of a quiet, kindly old man, shaking from the Parkinson's that had ravaged the temple of his magnificent body. But that kindly old man was once celebrated for his boxing prowess, then thrice reviled, first for his conversion to the Nation of Islam, then for the name change from Cassius Clay to Muhammad Ali, and finally for his refusal to be inducted into the U.S. Army on April 28, 1967. He, too, to steal a line from the great American poet Langston Hughes, *is* America. He was also, perhaps, the most famous person in the world, an American Muslim.

THE "PROBLEM," THIS BOOK'S SOLUTION, AND ITS AUTHOR

Muhammad Ali's life gave the lie to the "problem" that this book seeks to address, that Islam is viewed in a three-fold way: as new to America; as foreign to America; and as comprised of adherents who are violent, "un-American," and a threat to our nation. The reality, sketched in this book, is that Muslims have helped us to be *more* American, to be *better* Americans. Like Ali, we too, to return to the line from Hughes, *are* America. Think again of his marvelous poem "I, Too" which begins, "I, too, sing America. / I am the darker brother." We Muslim Americans are your darker brothers and sisters. At least one-quarter of us are African American, with roots in this country that go back to the transatlantic slave trade. A third of us are people like me, who are of South Asian ancestry, from Pakistan, India, or Bangladesh. A third of us are Middle Eastern, which may mean that we are Arab, but might also mean that we are Turkish, Kurdish, or Iranian. Some of us are White, some Latino/a, some biracial or of mixed heritage. The majority of us are Brown or Black. We, too, sing America. And though in the past, as Hughes describes, we have been sent to eat in the kitchen, Muslim Americans now affirm, in full voice, "Tomorrow, / I'll be at the table / When company comes. / . . . / They'll see how beautiful I am / And be ashamed— / I, too, am America."

I write these words as an American Muslim. I was born in Pakistan, and came to Canada when I was four. All of my education, kindergarten to PhD, was in Toronto. I wrote a dissertation at the University of Toronto on Muslim communities in Toronto, and in 1997 I did what many of my fellow Canadians have done in seeking greater glory. Like Joni Mitchell, Neil Young, and Leonard Cohen before me, I moved to Los Angeles. From 1997 to 2005, I taught in the California State University system. Since 2005, I have been teaching at Loyola Marymount University, the Jesuit university in Los Angeles. In 2013, after having been on a green card for almost a decade, I decided to become an American citizen. America is my home, where I have lived and worked for the past two decades. There is something almost mystical for me about the Constitution, and what it represents.

And like many immigrants, I wanted my part of the American dream as an American citizen. I, too, am America.

THE AMERICAN IDEAL

It is American to defend ourselves, to guard America against its foes. That's the oath I swore when I became an American citizen. There are other American ideals, to be sure. We are, to take only one example, producers of a culture that is consumed globally. American films, television, music, and literature are not just a domestic product, but valued around the world. We are not the most powerful country in the world because of our military, or because of our economy, but because of our cultural production. We have other ideals such as freedom, self-reliance, a unique and rugged individualism, industry, prosperity, and a reliance on God. It is from our religiosity that we get what is really at the heart of being American, which is to welcome the stranger, the marginalized. I saw this for myself in a beautiful way at a Rosh Hashanah service in Los Angeles in 2015. I was invited to the service by my friend, Rabbi Sharon Brous, who is the rabbi at IKAR, a wonderful center for Jewish renewal in Los Angeles. Sharon is one of the most influential rabbis in the United States, and the mayor of Los Angeles, Eric Garcetti, is a member of her congregation.

Before Sharon's sermon, Mayor Garcetti got up, and I thought he'd deliver the usual welcome that politicians do at such services. Instead, he did something that politicians rarely do when they have the microphone: he read a poem, "The New Colossus," by Emma Lazarus. It is the poem that is inscribed on the pedestal of the Statue of Liberty, our national symbol for welcoming the stranger. Its last lines speak to the truth and beauty of America, to our highest ideals:

"Give me your tired, your poor,
Your huddled masses yearning to breathe free,
The wretched refuse of your teeming shore.
Send these, the homeless, tempest-tost to me,
I lift my lamp beside the golden door!"

The mayor sat down, and Rabbi Brous began her sermon. She spoke of the Syrian refugee crisis, and the photograph of the drowned toddler, Alan Kurdi, that had shocked the world. She spoke of the need, the imperative, for us to welcome Syrian refugees. And she clearly wasn't speaking to me, as I was the only Muslim in the room. She was speaking to her thousand or so member congregation who had gathered together to celebrate the beginning of the Jewish new year. She reminded them of the painful history of discrimination that Jews had faced in America. Rabbi Brous told the story of the "St. Louis," the German ship loaded with Jewish refugees that was turned away from America in 1939. They were sent back to Europe, where many of them perished in the Holocaust. The "St. Louis" exemplified the darkest points in our history, and Rabbi Brous urged us not to repeat that example. It was an extraordinary moment of interfaith cooperation, at the beginning of the Jewish High Holy Days, to hear a sermon about the need to accept more refugees, many of them Muslim, into our country. This, too, *is* America.

ISLAM IN AMERICA

The history of Islam in America was captured in a nutshell in a speech made by President Barack Obama. On June 4, 2009, a few months into his presidency, President Obama spoke at Cairo University in Egypt. There, in the heart of the Arab world, he spoke about the history of Islam in America:

I also know that Islam has always been a part of America's story. The first nation to recognize my country was Morocco. In signing the Treaty of Tripoli in 1796, our second president, John Adams, wrote, "The United States has in itself no character of enmity against the laws, religion or tranquility of Muslims." And since our founding, American Muslims have enriched the United States. They have fought in our wars, they have served in our government, they have stood for civil rights, they have started businesses, they have taught at our universities, they've excelled in our sports arenas, they've won Nobel Prizes, built our tallest building, and lit the Olympic Torch. And when the first Muslim American was recently elected to Congress, he took the oath to defend our Constitution using the same Holy Koran that one of our Founding Fathers—Thomas Jefferson—kept in his personal library.

In this book, I discuss these claims made by President Obama, which highlight the contribution that Muslim Americans have made to America. We were here before America *was* America, arriving in slave ships bound for the colonies. To take only one example, in 1734 a biography was published in London about an African slave, sold in Annapolis, Maryland in 1730. Job ben Solomon was a Muslim, who attracted the attention of his owner because he could speak and read Arabic. The story of another African Muslim slave, Abdul Rahman Souri, was told in the 2007 PBS documentary *Prince among Slaves*, narrated by African American Muslim Hip Hop artist Mos Def. I first learned about this history of African Muslim slaves in 1977, when I stayed up to watch the television miniseries *Roots*. There, Alex Haley told the story of his family's roots, tracing themselves back to a slave named Kunta Kinte, who was also brought to Annapolis. In the series, Kunta Kinte was played by LeVar Burton, and I still remember the scenes of him speaking to his mentor, Fiddler (played by the extraordinary Louis Gossett Jr.), about his being a Muslim. Who knew that some of the slaves brought over from Africa were Muslims, who struggled to preserve their Muslim identity?

Historians estimate that between 10 and 20 percent of the slaves who came from West Africa were Muslim. Our third president, Thomas Jefferson, began learning Arabic in the 1770s, after he purchased a translation of the Qur'an in 1765. It was this Qur'an that Keith Ellison used when he was sworn in as the first Muslim member of Congress in 2007. In 1821 Mr. Jefferson wrote about freedom of religion extending to "the Jew and the Gentile, the Christian and Mahometan, the Hindoo and infidel of every denomination." Two hundred years later, the struggle for freedom, religious freedom, continues. America renews itself each time it stands for those whose freedom is threatened.

The first Muslim immigrants to North America other than slaves were from the Ottoman Empire in the late nineteenth century and the first half of the twentieth century. Many were itinerants who came to make money and then return to their countries of origin. Some, however, were farmers and merchants who settled permanently. Mosques sprang up in 1915 (Maine), 1919 (Connecticut), 1928 (New York), and 1929 (North Dakota). That's also important to remember: that there have been mosques in America for over a century.

In 1912 a Shi'a Muslim woman from Lebanon, Fatima Masselmany, boarded a ship in France that was sailing for America, taking her to her new home in Indiana. That would not be remarkable, except for the fact that the ship that she boarded was the Titanic. She survived the sinking of the Titanic, and made it to America, later moving from

Indiana to Michigan. Masselmany died in 1971, an American Muslim survivor of the Titanic.

In the last half-century, the Muslim population of the United States has increased dramatically through immigration, strong birth rates, and conversion. The Immigration and Nationality Act of 1965 allowed many more Muslims to immigrate than were previously allowed under the earlier quota system. America has in its past recognized and accepted Muslims. Through welcoming these Muslim strangers, we have become *more* American.

THIS BOOK

This book does not promise to mention, let alone discuss, every contribution of every American Muslim to the making of America. That would be a multivolume encyclopedia. This book hopes to mention a few representative figures, whose life and work exemplify many, many others whose names are recorded on voting rolls, whose children play organized sports, and who daily work in politics, civil service, business, or law. This book seeks to name a few as stand-ins for the many. The truth that this book seeks to cast some light upon—that Muslims, too, are America—does not demand a full accounting of every instance of Muslim impact. All that is required is to show that the fabric of America is woven, in part, with Muslim thread.

The first chapter gives a short history of Islam in America. The next three chapters look at particular contributions that American Muslims have made with respect to music, sports, and culture (broadly defined to include art, architecture, mosques, law, and politics). The concluding chapter makes the case that America would not be the country that it is without the contributions of Muslim Americans. Since, it is hoped, this book will be read both in and beyond academic institutions, there is a bibliographic note at the end with a list of sources consulted and suggestions for further reading.

1
Islam in America
A Short History

BEGINNINGS

We all come from somewhere. I don't mean that as a trite saying, or to state the obvious. I mean that as a statement of historical fact. Unless we are First Nations people (a preferred term for Native Americans, which, following Canadian usage, means the aboriginal or native people who were the first nations in North America), we came here from somewhere else, some much earlier than others. Muslims have been here long before America was America.

Of course, this begs the question of when America began, of when we can properly begin to speak of "America." Surely, it must be before our "official" birthdate, July 4, 1776. Do we date our beginnings to the mythological origins of the landing at Plymouth Harbor in November of 1620? Or do we push it back further, perhaps to that fateful day in 1492 when Columbus arrived on our shores? Whenever America begins, its founding bears connections to Islam and the Muslim world.

There are legendary stories of Muslim contact with North America. Some stories claim that Arab sailors "discovered" the continent five hundred years before Columbus. There are accounts of Arab historians such as Al-Masudi, who wrote in the tenth century about a sailor from Córdoba who returned from a journey across the Atlantic. In his map of the world from 956, Al-Masudi had that "unknown land" described by the sailor, across from the Atlantic.

Al-Masudi's World Map

Al-Idrisi, a twelfth-century historian who worked in the court of the king of Sicily, wrote about sailors who went from Portugal to the Caribbean, and had conversations in Arabic with the people they met. Abdullah Hakim Quick describes these encounters and others in his work, especially his book *Deeper Roots*. There are also stories of the empire of Mali sending ships across the Atlantic in the early 1300s, bringing with them both the Arabic and Mandinka languages. However, there is no hard evidence of this pre-Columbian contact, so the legends remain as tantalizing as they are unproven. They are lovely stories, and perhaps in the future there will be documentation discovered to support them. So let us instead move forward to where we have the scholarly evidence.

In 2012 we lost one of our most important scholars, María Rosa Menocal, the Sterling Professor of Humanities at Yale University. In her 1994 book *Shards of Love: Exile and the Origins of the Lyric*, she tells the story of Luis de Torres. Luis de Torres is little remembered now, but he was a *converso*, a Jew who was forced to convert to Christianity after the Reconquista began to strip Spain of its shared Jewish and Muslim heritage. Luis de Torres could speak Arabic (as well as Hebrew and Portuguese), and as such, he was valuable to Christopher Columbus, who in that same year of 1492 was planning his expedition. It is instructive to remember that at the same time that Columbus set sail, ships carrying Jews who refused to convert were also leaving the country—yet another form of exile for the Jewish people.

We know that Columbus thought he was sailing to India, not to the Americas. But he knew the usefulness of having an Arabic translator with him. If the people he met and wanted to trade with couldn't speak his language (Castilian, perhaps), or the formal language of his civilization (Latin), they would speak the *other* language of the civilized western world, Arabic. So an Arabic translator was brought on board, who had conversations with Taíno chiefs in Cuba. This begs the question of how those chiefs came into contact with Arabic speakers in the first place, a palimpsest perhaps of the evidence for pre-Columbian Arab contact described above. Menocal writes hauntingly about this conversation in *Shards of Love*, "the speaking of Arabic in the New World when in the Old it is being outlawed" (12). In

2007 there was controversy over the opening of an Arabic language school in Brooklyn (Khalil Gibran International Academy), with people unaware of the history of Arabic in the Americas. But of course it wasn't just the Arabic language that was brought to America, but Muslims and the religion of Islam as well.

AFRICAN SLAVES AND AMERICAN MUSLIMS

In 1528 a Muslim, Estevancio the Moor, landed in what is now Florida. He was a slave of Andrés Dorantes de Carranza, and they both accompanied the Spanish conquistador Pánfilo de Narváez on his expedition to the New World. Estevancio explored not only Florida but also Arizona, before he was killed in 1539 by the Zuni in what is now New Mexico. A Muslim, in other words, helped to explore and chart what would become the American south and west. That's one of the qualities we assign ourselves as Americans, explorers who open up new frontiers. Estevancio did just that, helping to do the work that would later open up the west. Almost eighty years before the Pilgrims landed in America, a Muslim slave had already died here.

Historians estimate that at least 10 percent of the slaves brought into colonial America from West Africa were Muslim. They literally helped to build America with their labor. In 2010, when controversy raged over the construction of the so-called "Ground Zero Mosque" in New York City, how many of us were aware of that fact? The mosque was planned for 51 Park Place, two blocks from the edge of the World Trade Center complex, and about six city blocks from the North Tower (the closer of the two towers to the mosque).

Masjid Manhattan was founded (on Warren Street) four blocks away from the World Trade Center months before the North Tower was completed, and a year before the South Tower was completed (in 1971). Each of the towers had a Muslim prayer room. I visited one of them the first time I came to New York City with my family in 1982. So there was a mosque in Lower Manhattan before the towers were finished, and each of the towers—whose very construction was made possible by an American Muslim engineer, Fazlur Rahman Khan—had a prayer space for Muslims.

The mosque was to have been built on the site of an abandoned Burlington Coat Factory, which at the time was already used as an overflow location for Masjid al-Farah, which moved to its current location (at 245 West Broadway) about twelve blocks from Ground Zero in 1985. I prayed in that space in the fall of 2011 on my first visit to the 9/11 Memorial.

By 2010 both Masjid Manhattan and Masjid al-Farah were over capacity, and had to turn people away. Both serve an immigrant Muslim community of South Asians and West Africans, as well as indigenous American Muslims, many of whom are in dire economic need. The Park 51 proposal was not only for a mosque, but a community center to provide social services to the needy in the area, both Muslim and non-Muslim.

While there was national and state opposition to the mosque, at the local level Manhattanites supported the mosque, 46 percent in favor to 36 percent against in a June 2010 poll, rising to 53 percent in favor to 31 percent against in August. Muslims, it may surprise us to learn, are part of the history of Lower Manhattan. One of the first Arab-American neighborhoods in New York City was Little Syria, built on Washington Street in the 1880s by Arab Muslims and Christians.

In 1991 the African Burial Grounds were discovered in Lower Manhattan, some six blocks from the proposed Park 51 mosque. The African Burial Ground National Monument on Duane Street in Lower Manhattan was proclaimed a National Monument in 2006 by President George W. Bush, and dedicated in 2007.

Eighteenth-century Wooden Ship at the 9/11 Site

In July 2010 the remains of a ship were found during the construction of the Ground Zero memorial. That September, at the New York Academy of Sciences, researchers described the boat as a sixty- to seventy-foot Hudson River sloop from the first half of the eighteenth century (1727–1760, based on a coin found on the ship), which "may have traveled up and down the Hudson River and perhaps the Atlantic seaboard, ferrying goods like sugar, molasses, salt and rum between the warm Caribbean and the uniting colonies to the north." That is a lovely pastoral image, until one remembers the Middle Passage, and that the "what" that was exchanged for the goods on that Hudson River sloop was not a "what" but a "who": slaves from West Africa, 10 percent of whom were Muslim, many of whom were buried in the soil of Lower Manhattan. Muslims are part of the history of Lower Manhattan.

For most of American history, Muslims have come to New York seeking freedom and opportunity—like every other group of immigrants—another of our American ideals. In 1847, for example, sailor and slave Mahommah Baquaqua escaped from the Brazilian ship *Lembranca*, docked in Manhattan. *The Biography of Mahommah G. Baquaqua* describes how when confined to a cell on the *Lembranca*, Baquaqua broke down the door, bowed to the wife of his owner, and ran away. Once on the docks, he uttered the only English word he knew: "free." What could be more representative of the American ideal of freedom than that? And Muslims were among those killed in the terrorist attacks of 9/11. If it is the dead who make Ground Zero sacred, then that sacredness includes the Muslim dead.

Ayuba Sulciman Diallo (1701–1773), also known as Job ben Solomon, was another Muslim who was brought as a slave to Annapolis in 1730. This, one needs to remember, was two years before George Washington was born. Annapolis was the same city where twenty years after Solomon's arrival, another Muslim slave, Kunta Kinte, the ancestor of Alex Haley, was brought and sold. Solomon's story was told in a slave narrative that was published in London in 1734. That story was written by Rev. Thomas Bluett, who was impressed that this captured slave knew Arabic. Once Solomon gained his freedom, he came to England in 1733, on his way back to Africa. In England, he met with notable political and business figures. So forty years before the American Revolution would begin, people in England knew about Muslim slaves in the colonies.

And there are numerous other slave narratives, some of which talk about enslaved Muslim women. In 1991 Julie Dash released her independent film *Daughters of the Dust*, the first feature-length film directed by an African American woman to be distributed in theaters across the United States. The film told the story of three generations of Gullah women. The Gullah were Africans, some of whom were Muslim, who were enslaved in Georgia and South Carolina. Amir Muhammad has documented some of these stories of Gullah women at his Islamic Heritage Museum and Cultural Center in Washington, D.C.

In 2008 Unity Productions Foundation produced a documentary for PBS entitled *Prince among Slaves* (from the same-titled book by Terry Alford). That documentary, narrated by American Muslim Hip Hop artist Mos Def, told the story of Abdul Rahman Ibrahima Sori, captured by Mandinka slavers in 1787 and brought to Natchez, Mississippi, where he remained a slave until 1828.

At the Philadelphia Museum of Art, one can see the portrait of yet another American Muslim, Yarrow Mamout (Muhammad Yaro) painted in 1819 by Charles Willson Peale. Mamout was a freed slave from Guinea who lived in Georgetown, D.C., and was approximately seventy-seven years old when Peale painted his portrait. Peale noted in his diary that Mamout was a success, "comfortable in his Situation having Bank stock and [he] lives in his own house."

MR. JEFFERSON, THE BARBARY COAST, AND ISLAM

If you don't know the story of Yarrow Mamout, you are certainly familiar with our first president, General George Washington. Among General Washington's possessions

Portrait of Yarrow Mamout
by Charles Willson Peale

were his slaves, two of them named Fatima and Little Fatima (presumed to be the daughter of Fatima). So our first president, the father of our country, owned Muslim slaves, who helped to build Mount Vernon. Or think of our third president, Thomas Jefferson. Jefferson wrote his own epitaph, which was carved into his gravestone in Monticello: "Here was buried Thomas Jefferson, author of the Declaration of American Independence, of the Statute of Virginia for Religious Freedom, and father of the University of Virginia." Any one of those would be a tremendous accomplishment for one of our founding fathers. To have achieved all three is extraordinary.

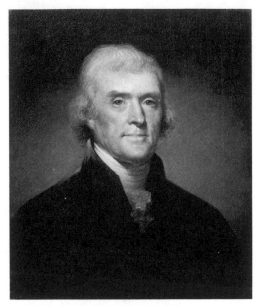

Portrait of Thomas Jefferson
by Rembrandt Peale

In drafting the legal documents that were crucial to the history of our country, Jefferson took an interest in comparative politics and comparative religion. Given the conflict between European and Muslim empires, it was no surprise that he took an interest in Islam. To be clear, Jefferson was no fan of Islam. But he purchased a Qur'an in 1765, the translation by George Sale. The story of this Qur'an is described in Denise Spellberg's carefully researched book *Thomas Jefferson's Qur'an*. It was this Qur'an that Keith Ellison used in a private ceremony after he was sworn in as the first Muslim member of Congress in 2007.

There was controversy over this ceremony, as some conservative commentators insisted that Ellison be sworn in on a Bible. However, that would be a religious test, and one

THE

K O R A N,

COMMONLY CALLED

The Alcoran *of* MOHAMMED,

Tranflated into ENGLISH immediately from
the Original ARABIC;

WITH

EXPLANATORY NOTES,

TAKEN FROM THE MOST

APPROVED COMMENTATORS,

TO WHICH IS PREFIXED,

A Preliminary Difcourfe.

VOL. I.

By GEORGE SALE, Gent.

Nulla falfa doctrina eft, quae non aliquid veri permifceat.
Auguftin. Quaeft. Evang. l. ii. c. xl.

LONDON,

Printed for L. HAWES, W. CLARKE, and R. COLLINS, at the
Red Lion in Pater Nofter Row; and T. WILCOX, at Virgil's
Head, overagainft the New Church, in the Strand.
MDCCLXIV.

*Title Page
of Thomas Jefferson's Qur'an*

of our American ideals is that one can belong to any religious tradition (or no religious tradition at all) and still hold office. New members of Congress are sworn in en masse by the Speaker of the House, and they may hold in their hands whatever texts they choose. After the official ceremony, they usually have another ceremony in their offices that will be photographed for publicity purposes. So Keith Ellison lived out one of our highest American ideals of religious freedom.

To return to our origins, a decade before 1776, the man who would write the Declaration of Independence and become the new country's third president, read the Qur'an.

Swearing-in Ceremony for Keith Ellison

While I don't want to make too much of this point—Mr. Jefferson, to repeat myself, was no fan of Islam—his owning a copy of the Qur'an and reading it is crucial to my argument that Islam is part of the history of America. That argument is strengthened when we realize that Jefferson also began to teach himself Arabic in the 1770s. Jefferson wasn't phenomenal at Arabic (he was self-taught, after all), but as with most things he did, he was pretty good.

The religious freedom that was central to early America was enshrined in the 1777 Virginia Statute for Religious Freedom. Part of that is inscribed on the northwest portico of the Jefferson Memorial in Washington, D.C.: "Almighty God hath created the mind free. All attempts to influence it by temporal punishments or burthens . . . are a departure from the plan of the holy Author of our religion . . . No man shall be compelled to frequent or support religious worship or ministry or shall otherwise suffer on account of his religious opinions or belief, but all men shall be free to profess and by argument to maintain, their opinions in matters of religion." And lest one think that Jefferson was speaking of religious freedom only for Christians, he wrote in his autobiography in 1821 about freedom of religion extending to "the Jew and the Gentile, the Christian and Mahometan [Muslim], the Hindoo and infidel of every denomination."

In President Obama's 2009 speech about Islam in America, he spoke about the 1797 Treaty of Peace and Friendship between the United States of America and the Bey and Subjects of Tripoli of Barbary. Authored by diplomat Joel Barlow in 1796, it was approved by the Senate on June 7, 1797, and signed and proclaimed three days later by our second president, John Adams. Article 11 of the treaty reads:

> As the government of the United States of America is not in any sense founded on the Christian Religion; as it has in itself no character of enmity against the laws, religion or tranquility of Mussulmen [Muslims]; and as the said States never have entered into any war or act of hostility against any Mahometan [Muslim] nation, it is declared by the parties that no pretext arising from religious opinions shall ever produce an interruption of the harmony existing between the two countries.

It is an extraordinary treaty, declaring first that the government of the United States is not founded on Christianity. This contradicts current attempts to understand our founding as a Christian or "Judeo-Christian" country. Second, the treaty affirms that the United States has as a principle no issue with the practice of Islam, and has not entered into hostilities with any Muslim countries. The backdrop to this treaty of peace and friendship is the conflict between the newly formed United States and the Barbary Coast pirates. In that sense, the founding of the modern American Navy is connected to the Muslim world.

We created a navy to fight the Revolutionary War against the British. With the defeat of the British, we no longer needed a navy to protect our coasts. However, as a new country, we needed to protect our trade routes and shipping lanes. The 2013 film *Captain Phillips*, starring Tom Hanks, dealt with the current reality of Somali pirates. However, pirates have been at work along the east coast of Africa since the first ships laden with goods sailed those waters. In our early days as a colonial outpost of Britain, the British government paid tribute to the Barbary Coast pirates, guaranteeing safe passage for our ships. Governments, contrary to some public proclamations, often negotiate with terrorists. With their defeat in the Revolutionary War, the British government had no reason to continue to make these payments. As a new country, saddled with the debts of that war, we had no money to pay that tribute either. So we reconstituted our navy to protect our shipping lanes.

Crypt of John Paul Jones, U.S. Naval Academy

The basement of the chapel at the U.S. Naval Academy in Annapolis contains a marvelous crypt for the remains of John Paul Jones, the "father" of the modern American Navy. Think for a moment about the "Marine Hymn," since the Marines are part of the Navy. I play it for my students to help them understand the connections between the beginnings of our American institutions and the Muslim world. The students all know why the song begins with the words "From the halls of Montezuma. . . ." Our campus is some three hours from Mexico, and our students are quite familiar with the history of that particular border. But they are usually stumped when I ask them why the next words are there: ". . . to the shores of Tripoli." They are unaware

Tripoli Monument, Annapolis, Maryland

of the connection in early American history with Libya and Muslims. I need to remind them of the wars with the Barbary Coast pirates, wars that were engaged in by John Paul Jones, wars that resulted in our modern Navy.

When asked, most Americans probably could not name the oldest military monument in the United States. It is the Tripoli Monument, created for the war against the Barbary Coast pirates in 1804, and carved in Italy in 1806. The Tripoli Monument was installed in the Navy Yard in 1808 and moved to its current location at the Naval Academy in 1860.

Detail of the Tripoli Monument

The pirates on the Tripoli Monument may well be the first images of Muslims to be found in America. One sees them with their mustaches, turbans, and crossed scimitars. It is as stereotypical an image of "the Turk" as one could hope to find at the beginning of the nineteenth century.

Over a century later, an image of the Prophet Muhammad, holding both a sword and a Qur'an, was added to a frieze on the walls of the U.S. Supreme Court. This was to celebrate "the great lawgivers of history," and included images of other religious figures, Moses, Solomon, and Confucius.

The Prophet Muhammad, U.S. Supreme Court

EARLY AMERICAN MUSLIMS

It wasn't always a violent confrontation that defined the early relationships between the United States and the Muslim world. The first Muslim immigrants to America who weren't slaves were "Turks," from the Ottoman Empire. They included Albanians, Arabs, Kurds, and Turks, who emigrated in the late nineteenth century and the first half of the twentieth century. Many were itinerants who came to make money and then return to their countries of origin. Some, however, settled permanently and built institutions.

It is instructive to remember that we have had mosques in this country, structures built and used exclusively as mosques, for over a century. The first of these mosques was in Biddeford, Maine. In the 1890s the town was home to two large textile mills, which both recruited foreign workers. The Pepperell textile mill recruited workers from Albania, who were Muslim. They built the first mosque in America in 1915.

In the nineteenth century, there were also American converts to Islam. The most famous was Alexander Russell Webb. Umar F. Abd-Allah, one of our most important contemporary American Muslim scholars, has written the definitive biography of Webb, *A Muslim in Victorian America: The Life of Alexander Russell Webb*. Webb was born in Massachusetts in 1846 and became a prominent journalist. He was appointed as ambassador to the Philippines in 1887, and it was there that he came to learn about Islam through the writings of Mirza Ghulam Ahmad. A year later, he made his conversion and became a Muslim. Webb traveled to India, Egypt, and Turkey to learn more about Islam, and his wife and children also converted. When Webb returned to the United States, he also returned to his journalistic roots, publishing a short-lived journal about Islam, the *Moslem World*, which ran for seven months. This monthly journal was designed to spread Islam to an American audience. Webb also published a small book, *Islam in America*, from the publishing company that he established in New York. In order to advance this missionary work, Webb spoke about Islam at the first World Parliament of Religions in 1893 in Chicago. He also set up a mosque in Manhattan. Given Webb's prominence in journalism and politics, he was able to reach a number of Americans, perhaps including Mark Twain. Webb's work as a journalist had been in Missouri, where Twain had gotten his start decades earlier. Of the connection between the two, Abd-Allah writes,

Webb apparently knew Twain and personally invited him and several other dignitaries to one of his first highly publicized parlor talks on Islam in February 1893. . . . Mark Twain knew of Webb's mission, and his well-known reference to 'Missouri Moslems' in *Tom Sawyer Abroad*, which appeared in 1894, a year after the parliament, may well have been written with Webb in mind and probably evoked images of Webb for many American readers of the book in the 1890s. (12)

Webb died in 1916 and was buried in Lyndhurst, New Jersey, an early American Muslim journalist, politician, and religious proselytizer.

THE NATION OF ISLAM AND MALCOLM X

Given the historical beginnings of American Islam with African slaves, it's not surprising that one of the early American Muslim movements began with African Americans. This is the Nation of Islam (NOI), a uniquely American Muslim movement. The roots of the NOI can be traced to the growing interest in Africa at the beginning of the twentieth century. People were beginning to challenge the stereotypes of Africa being uncivilized, a "dark continent." Into this came one of the precursors to the NOI, Marcus Garvey (d. 1940) and the Universal Negro Improvement Association (UNIA) that he organized in Jamaica in 1914. Garvey was a proponent of Pan-Africanism and, as the name of his organization implied, of improving the lives of Black people. In 1916 he moved to America, and formed a UNIA chapter in New York. Part of Garvey's plan was for Black people to return home to Africa, since he believed they would only face continued discrimination in the United States. The goal was to return to Liberia, but that never materialized.

Another movement around the same time was that of Noble Drew Ali (1886–1929) and the Moorish Science Temple of America (1913). Ali took a different approach than Garvey. Given objections to the term "Negro" by some people, Ali instead referred to African Americans as "Asiatics," and claimed descent from the Moors, with an affinity for Morocco. And unlike Garvey, Ali saw his members as being loyal American citizens, with no reason to leave their country. In fact, the identity card carried by members ended with the line "I am a citizen of the USA." He set up the first temple in New Jersey, and then moved to various places, ending up in Chicago where he set up Temple No. 9 in 1926. Ali's followers took the surname of "El," or "Bey" or "Ali," to signify their identity as Moors. One still sees this legacy in modern America, with for example the name of a former Pittsburgh Steelers wide receiver, Antwaan Randle El.

While Ali had his followers read a text called the *Holy Koran of the Moorish Science Temple of America*, it had no connection to the Qur'an read by Muslims. Instead, Ali's *Koran* was a combination of his own writings, *The Aquarian Gospel of Jesus the Christ*, and a Rosicrucian work. However, there were Islamic themes and symbols in the group, and the identity card contained the lines "The Blessings of the God of our Father, Allah, be upon you that carry this card. I do hereby declare that you are a Moslem under the Divine Laws of the Holy Koran of Mecca, Love, Truth, Peace, Freedom and Justice."

These two organizations, the Universal Negro Improvement Association, and the Moorish Science Temple of America, influenced the Nation of Islam. Wallace D. Fard (also known as Wallace Fard Muhammad), a peddler of goods, appeared in Detroit in 1930. There were rumors that he was a member of the Moorish Science Temple, and had left as a result of a split in the movement after the death of Noble Drew Ali. This came on the heels of the Great Migration, where African Americans moved from the rural south to the urban north, so that the African American population of Detroit, for example, increased some twenty-fold between 1910 and 1920. Fard preached a message that resonated with some African Americans, that they were good, and that the White people oppressing them were evil. He told people that Christianity was the religion of the White slave master, imposed upon the African slave, that the true religion of Black people was Islam, and that he was a messenger sent from Allah to bring these truths to the Lost Found Nation of Islam in America. He founded the first temple in Detroit, and in 1931 made a convert of Elijah Poole. Fard renamed Elijah as Elijah Karriem, and then later as Elijah Muhammad. This was one of Fard's gifts as a prophet, that he could give people their "true" names, which had been stolen from them with the imposition of the name given to them by their slave masters. Elijah Muhammad established the second temple in Chicago, spreading the movement.

Fard disappeared in 1934, and Elijah Muhammad began to preach that Fard *was* Allah who had appeared in the flesh, and that he was now the Messenger of Allah. On the surface, it sounded Islamic; Muhammad was the Messenger of Allah. But the Allah was a human person, and the Muhammad was born in Sandersville, Georgia, not Arabia. Some of the ideology of the Nation of Islam was positive, telling African Americans to love themselves, and take control of their own lives and economic affairs. Other parts of the ideology were quite negative, with White people literally being the devil, devilish creations of an evil scientist exiled by the wise Black leaders of original humanity. In 1942 Elijah

Muhammad was sentenced to prison for not registering for the draft in World War II, and for encouraging his followers neither to register for the draft, nor to serve in the armed forces. This would come back some twenty-five years later when another member, Muhammad Ali, refused to serve in the Vietnam War.

The Nation of Islam received a boost when a young man named Malcolm Little (born in Omaha in 1925) joined them while he was in prison in 1948. The NOI did a lot of prison outreach, and Malcolm's brother Reginald had already joined the group and spoken about it to Malcolm. Malcolm would go on to become one of the most important figures in twentieth-century America.

In January of 2015, I flew into Omaha to drive out to the Malcolm X birth site in North Omaha. The drive in itself was interesting, yet another reminder that, fifty years after Malcolm's assassination, the "two solitudes" of racial segregation are still very much with us in America. The night before, I was in the renovated Old Market area of downtown Omaha. In an eight-block area, wandering around for several hours, I saw only one Black face, the African American gentleman seated beside me at the dinner counter of a lovely French restaurant. Driving the three miles the next morning to North Omaha, it was *only* Black folks that I saw.

It was lovely to see the historical marker at the site, surrounded by a park that will be developed, but I thought it needed so much more. You wouldn't know the birth site/memorial was there unless you were looking for it. There was no sign of it from the road. A quiet morning, with just me and the wild turkeys (I think that's what they were. I'm a city kid so the only birds I know are pigeons, and these were far too big to be pigeons) wandering around the site. I don't think we remember Malcolm enough, or give him his rightful due in American history.

His story has been described in his own autobiography, as well as in the magisterial biography by the late Manning Marable, *Malcolm X: A Life of Reinvention*. Malcolm's rise in the Nation of Islam has been well documented, most notably his establishment of temples in Boston, Springfield, Hartford, and Atlanta. It peaked in 1959 when Mike Wallace did a television profile on him and the NOI for WTNA in New York. The following year, at the United Nations General Assembly, Malcolm met with world leaders including Gamal Abdel Nasser of Egypt, and Fidel Castro of Cuba.

In 1964 Malcolm broke publicly with the Nation of Islam, and became a Sunni Muslim. He also made his famous pilgrimage to Mecca that year, where he denounced the racial teachings of the NOI. He was assassinated the following year by men who were members of the NOI.

Malcolm's was the classic self-help or "pull yourself up by your bootstraps" American story. He didn't know his father, was raised by a single mom, and turned to crime to support himself. In jail, he found religion, and turned his life around. If the religion he had found had been Christianity, I'm convinced that we'd be speaking now of Saint Malcolm. But the religion that he found, first, was the Nation of Islam. That scared a lot of people with its racial teachings, but it also taught young Black men to love themselves—to stop eating unhealthy food, stop drinking alcohol, stop doing drugs, and stop being sexually promiscuous. Given the enormous problems that young men, particularly young Black and Brown men, face in our inner cities and prisons, Malcolm's example was extraordinary. In an age when the United States incarcerates more people than any other country on earth, Malcolm's thoughts and insights on how to help young people are sorely needed.

After his break from the NOI, Malcolm found Sunni Islam, and became El-Hajj Malik El-Shabazz. His wife, Betty Shabazz, was a mentor to countless young women and men, especially at Medgar Evers College, where she worked until her death in 1997. They renounced the racism of the NOI and were working as part of the civil rights movement. No less an American icon than Stan Lee has talked about how part of his inspiration for the X-Men comics (which are now incredibly popular movies) was in the connection between Dr. Martin Luther King Jr. and Malcolm X. So one has Professor Charles Xavier wanting harmonious coexistence and Magneto wanting separation. It's Martin and Malcolm told in comic form with mutants taking the roles of Black people. American theologian James Cone has written about their intertwined legacies in his book *Martin & Malcolm & America: A Dream or a Nightmare*. That's important to remember that Malcolm was just as influential a leader for civil rights as Dr. King.

AFTER MALCOLM

A decade later, after the death of Elijah Muhammad in 1975, his son Wallace D. Muhammad took over the Nation, and brought the majority of its members into Sunni orthodoxy. He changed his own name to Warith Deen Mohammed. A number of splinter groups emerged, and on November 8, 1977, Louis Farrakhan declared his intention to reestablish the Nation of Islam according to the principles of the Honorable Elijah Muhammad. Warith Deen Mohammed is important to mention here, as one of the most important American Muslim leaders at the end of the twentieth century.

June 28, 1952, saw the first national Muslim conference in Cedar Rapids, Iowa, with four hundred Muslims from Canada and the United States in attendance. In July of 1954, the Federation of Islamic Associations of the United States and Canada (FIA) was formed. The first conference of the FIA was held a year later in London, Ontario. These conferences are important because they mark the beginnings of the national institutionalization of Islam in America.

With the growth of the Muslim community in North America, and the migration of Muslim students from other countries (particularly the Arab world, but also Iran, India, Pakistan, and Turkey) to study in North America, the Muslim Students Association (MSA) was formed in 1963. Today, there are active chapters of the MSA in most major colleges and universities in North America.

Out of the MSA, the Islamic Society of North America (ISNA) was created in 1982. It is the largest Islamic organization in North America, with its headquarters (including a large mosque) in Plainfield, Indiana. The ISNA convention, held every year around the Labor Day weekend, often in Chicago, is the largest annual American gathering of Muslims. ISNA has encouraged Muslims in North America to develop more extensive links with their local communities, including full participation in the American political process.

There are concerns about Muslim refugees from the Middle East, especially in light of the war in Iraq and the destabilization of Syria. But we have had Muslims come to America from the Middle East for some two centuries. One of the most famous early ones was Hajji Ali (also known as Hi Jolly), who probably came from Egypt in 1856 with a group of camels that were ordered by Jefferson Davis (yes, *that* Jefferson Davis) a year earlier to help open up the

American southwest. The camels, unfortunately, could not negotiate the rocky ground of Texas, and so the experiment was halted, but Ali continued to work for the U.S. Army.

Since that time, there have been numerous Muslims who have come from the Middle East to America. One thinks of people as diverse as Ahmed Zewail, born in Egypt and winning the Nobel Prize in chemistry at Caltech, or Shirin Neshat from Iran, who lives in New York and has won awards for her art and her films. American Muslims, including those from the Middle East, have helped us to be better Americans, winning major prizes around the world, advancing both knowledge and cultural production.

2
Blues for Allah
Music

In 2007 Kid Rock (born Robert Ritchie) released his seventh studio record, *Rock N Roll Jesus*. The record debuted at number one on the Billboard chart, the first and only of Kid Rock's records to do so. The third single, "All Summer Long," released a year later, was a worldwide hit. The song name-checked and sampled the Lynyrd Skynyrd classic "Sweet Home Alabama," as iconic an American rock song as there is. The CD booklet closed with a picture of Kid Rock and a man who had died the year before, with the moving caption "In loving memory of my dear friend Ahmet M. Ertegun." On the opposite page of the booklet, in the time-honored tradition of liner notes, Kid Rock ended his with the simple phrase, "All praise be to God." That's a phrase that people of many religious traditions can say, especially those who are Christian or Muslim. And perhaps Kid Rock learned that phrase from Ertegun, who certainly knew and spoke it in its Arabic form, *alhamdulillah*, "all praise is due to God."

IN LOVING MEMORY OF MY DEAR FRIEND
AHMET M. ERTEGUN

Kid Rock's Tribute to Ahmet Ertegun

Ahmet Ertegun died at the age of eighty-three on December 14, 2006, from complications arising from a fall a few weeks earlier. However, unlike other eighty-year-olds who tragically often suffer a similar fate, Ertegun sustained his injury in the VIP area before a concert with The Rolling Stones at the Beacon Theatre in New York City. I haven't yet reconciled myself to dying. But since eventually I am going to die, to do so on my beloved Upper West Side, at a pre-show VIP party for one of a pair of Stones concerts that would be filmed by Martin Scorsese and released as the documentary *Shine a Light* (which was dedicated to Ertegun's memory), is a pretty good way to shuffle off this mortal coil. Ahmet Ertegun, the president and cofounder of Atlantic Records and the chairman of the Rock and Roll Hall of Fame, a man who shaped the music of the twentieth century—not just in America, but around the world—was an American Muslim. It is to him, and to Muhammad Ali, perhaps the two American Muslims with the greatest global influence, that this book is dedicated.

Ertegun came from a very important Turkish Muslim family. His great grandfather, Shaikh Ibrahim Effendi, was the head of a distinguished Sufi order in Istanbul, the Özbekler Tekkesi. It was to this "Uzbek Tekke," the headquarters of the Sufi fraternity, that Ertegun's body was taken back for burial with his family members. Ertegun's father, Mehmet Munir Ertegun, was an advisor to Ataturk, and the second ambassador of the Republic of Turkey to the United States. He served from 1934 to 1944, but when he died of a heart attack in 1944, there was no mosque in D.C. that could hold his funeral, and his body could not be returned to Turkey due to the fighting of World War II. As a result, after World War II, the Islamic Center of Washington was built. It was this mosque, coincidentally, that President George W. Bush visited on September 17, 2001, a demonstration in the week after the 9/11 attacks of his solidarity with American Muslims. In 1946 Munir Ertegun's body was taken back to his native Turkey aboard the USS Missouri, the very same battleship that had been the place of the signing of the Japanese surrender on September 2, 1945, marking the end of World War II. That it was the USS Missouri which brought Ambassador Ertegun's body home, delivering it with full honors including the firing of the ship's guns, was an indication of the respect in which he was held, and of the relationship between the United States and Turkey. The Cold War would soon begin, and the United States needed Turkey as an ally against the Soviet Union.

Ahmet Ertegun moved to Washington, D.C. in 1935, when he was twelve years old. That year, according to Robert Greenfield's biography *The Last Sultan: The Life of Ahmet Ertegun*, Ertegun became the first person to ask an unknown young singer for her autograph. That woman would later gain recognition as an American treasure, the First Lady of Song, Ella Fitzgerald. Prior to coming to America, Ertegun had lived in London, where his father had been an ambassador to the Court of St. James' for two years. It was as a child in London, influenced by both his mother and his older brother Nesuhi, that Ertegun began his lifelong fascination with American music. He heard the likes of Duke Ellington and Cab Calloway when they performed in London, leading to his meeting with Lady Ella a few years later after one of her early performances with the Chick Webb Orchestra. Given his musical interests, it was no surprise that the young Ahmet found himself often in the Black areas of D.C., most notably around the Howard University campus. In the staid White D.C. of the 1940s, the action was in the Black neighborhoods. As a Turkish Muslim, he also saw a connection with Black Americans, both of whom were marginalized in America—Blacks because of their race, Turks because of their religion.

Ahmet and Nesuhi hosted parties that were integrated, something quite unusual for that time and that place in America. The brothers sometimes booked Jazz concerts at the Jewish Community Center, one of the few places at that time that allowed "race mixing." When their father died, Ahmet stayed in D.C., where he was studying philosophy at Georgetown University. With his friend Herb Abrahamson and a $10,000 loan from their dentist, Ahmet cofounded Atlantic Records in 1947. A few years later, they had their first big hit, Granville "Stick" McGhee's "Drinkin' Wine Spo-Dee-O-Dee." Atlantic Records became famous in the 1950s for their Rhythm and Blues sides, recording artists such as Big Joe Turner, Ruth Brown, La Vern Baker, and

Professor Longhair. In 1952 Atlantic Records signed the Genius, Ray Charles. His first hit for Atlantic came in 1953, a song written by Ahmet Ertegun himself, "Mess Around." The Genius stayed with Atlantic until 1959, releasing "What'd I Say" with the label. I am not a musicologist, but I'd argue that "What'd I Say" was the song that made Ray Charles appeal as much to White audiences as to Black ones. It can also be argued that it was the first Soul recording, something in which Atlantic Records would specialize in the 1960s, in the same way they had worked in Rhythm and Blues in the 1950s.

In 1991, when I was a PhD student at the University of Toronto, I received a prestigious national scholarship for graduate work. I celebrated by buying myself a present, one I had coveted since its release in 1985 but couldn't afford as a student. It was the Atlantic Rhythm and Blues 1947—1974 box set, seven double records of the most important sides that had been recorded on Atlantic. The Allmusic.com site highlighted the importance of this set, writing that it "should be a part of any collection that presumes to take American music—not just rock & roll or rhythm & blues—seriously." I knew about the importance of Atlantic Records to American music, but I had no idea of the importance of Ahmet Ertegun to Atlantic Records until I bought this set. I had no idea that he was a Muslim until I began to do further research into his life.

Some who knew about Ahmet's lifestyle might interject that he wasn't a "good" Muslim. He lived the high life, was a bon vivant, drank, partied to excess, and had numerous affairs. But of course, there are lots of Muslims who do things that we are not supposed to do as Muslims. We sometimes think of all Muslims as "Hasidic Muslims," a term used by my friend Rabbi Reuven Firestone. Reuven means this to say that we think of all Muslims as "practicing" or "orthodox" Muslims, men with long beards and covered heads who are scrupulous in their observance of the most conservative form of Islamic law. We don't think of the "secular" Muslims, who are as much a part of American life as secular Jews or Christians. The majority of American Muslims, it surprises some people to learn, are not affiliated with any mosque. I live in Los Angeles, where the largest religious population, not surprisingly, is Catholics. The second-largest religious population is ex-Catholics. We should not be surprised, then, that there are lapsed Muslims, nonobservant Muslims, and different types of observant Muslims. American Muslims, just like Christians or Jews, are not, and have never been, a homogeneous group.

What is crucial here is that it was an American Muslim, Ahmet Ertegun, who had a profound impact on American society, not just on American music. He came of age in the racial discrimination of America in the 1930s and 1940s. He identified the religious discrimination he faced as a Muslim with the racial discrimination faced by African Americans. And he did what he could to challenge that, to bring people together, figuratively in listening to music, literally at parties and concerts. In the 1940s very few White people listened to "Race" music, as Black music was known then. In the 1950s all Americans, not just African Americans, were listening to Ray Charles, thanks to Ahmet Ertegun and Atlantic Records.

The Soul sides that Atlantic Records released in the 1960s, beginning with "Green Onions" by Booker T. and the MG's in 1962, continued this trend of shared culture and shared life through shared music. We cannot properly understand American music in the twentieth century without the contributions of the Drifters, Ben E. King, the

Immortal Otis Redding, Sam and Dave, the Wicked Wilson Pickett, or the Queen of Soul, Aretha Franklin. In our racial divides, it is often music that brings us together, helping us to transcend our differences. It was Atlantic Records, and Ahmet Ertegun, who released some of the most important work by these African American artists. And if changing the face of American music wasn't enough, Ahmet turned his attention to other shores. He signed Led Zeppelin to Atlantic Records, and was responsible for the distribution of the records released by The Rolling Stones. He was Chairman of the Rock and Roll Hall of Fame, and was inducted into the Hall in 1987. He also played a significant role in American sport. Ahmet, his brother Nesuhi, and Steve Ross cofounded the New York Cosmos of the North American Soccer League. It was the Cosmos who brought the greatest ever to play that game, Pelé, to New York in 1975. In 2000 Ertegun was named a Living Legend by the Library of Congress. According to the Library's website, the "professional accomplishments of the Living Legends have enabled them to provide examples of personal excellence that have benefited others and enriched the nation in a variety of ways."

MUSLIM ROOTS OF THE BLUES

Although Ahmet Ertegun was the American Muslim who provided the most influence on American music, the story of American Muslims and American music did not begin with him. For those beginnings, we have to go back to the transatlantic slave trade. One of our finest historians of that time is Sylviane Diouf, who directs the Lapidus Center for the Historical Analysis of Transatlantic Slavery at the Schomburg Center for Research in Black Culture of the New York Public Library. The director of the Schomburg

Center since 2011, incidentally, has been Khalil Gibran
Muhammad, a great grandson of Elijah Muhammad, one
of the leading figures in the Nation of Islam. That is yet
another example of the connections between American
Muslims and American culture.

We know that one of the roots of American Blues music
is West African Blues. Professor Diouf makes the connection, via the transatlantic slave trade, to West African Islam.
She gives a presentation on "Muslim Roots of the Blues,"
where she begins by playing the Muslim call to prayer. She
then plays a field recording of "Levee Camp Holler," one
of the early recorded Mississippi Delta Blues songs. It's the
same melody, nasal intonations, and note changes in both
songs. Professor Diouf doesn't think this is coinciden-
tal, but rather the product of West African Muslims being
enslaved in the Americas. It's no surprise that the music
they performed, as Muslims, came to influence the music
they performed as Americans. Often, scholars recognize
things as "African" in origin, but don't make the link to
their specifically Islamic origins in Africa. So, for example,
Jonathan David published an extraordinary book, *Together
Let Us Sweetly Live*, about the singing and praying bands in
the African Methodist Episcopal Churches in the Delaware
and Chesapeake Bays. One of the key features of this worship is to set up a mourner's bench, and circumambulate it
counterclockwise. This, of course, is what the pilgrims do at
the Ka'ba in Mecca. These are subtle traces, to be sure, but
traces nonetheless that show the impact of Islamic practices
on African American worship and music.

BLUES FOR ALLAH

There's also an interesting connection with the Blues to
an important American band, the Grateful Dead. In 1975

the Dead released their eighth studio record, the intriguingly titled *Blues for Allah*. In 1975 it was unusual for an American record to have "Allah" in the title, let alone to have a track on said record with the same name. The Dead only played "Blues for Allah" in 1975, and I couldn't find any evidence of it having been played after that. The song ends with the lines "blues for Allah / Insha'allah," with *insha'allah* being a common phrase used by Muslims, "if God wills." The lyricist for the Dead, Robert Hunter, has written about this song in his book of lyrics, *Box of Rain*:

> This lyric is a requiem for King Faisal of Saudi Arabia, a progressive and democratically inclined ruler (and, incidentally, a fan of the Grateful Dead) whose assassination in 1975 shocked us personally. The lyrics were printed in Arabic on the jacket of the Middle Eastern release of the album. (20)

I was intrigued by this, especially the idea that King Faisal was a fan. I tried to get in touch with Robert Hunter to ask him if he would speak with me about this song. Unfortunately, Hunter politely refused, as he always does when asked about his lyrics or meanings. But it is interesting to see an iconic American band, long before the revolution in Iran or the Soviet invasion of Afghanistan, influenced by Islamic themes and by events happening in the Muslim world. Three years later, the Dead would play three shows at the Pyramids in Giza, Egypt. There, they jammed with Egyptian musicians, including the legendary Nubian oud player, Hamza El-Din, who spent most of his life after those performances living in Oakland, California. Hamza El-Din was crucial in the development of "world music" in the 1980s, yet another contribution by an American Muslim not just to American music, but to music around the world.

ALLAH SUPREME: JAZZ AND AMERICAN MUSLIMS

Another influence of American Muslims on American music was in the realm of Jazz. This was done through a heterodox Muslim group, the Ahmadiyya (also known as Ahmadis). The Ahmadi community takes its name from Mirza Ghulam Ahmad (1835–1908), who lived in what was then India. According to a pamphlet published by the community (entitled *Who Are Ahmadi Muslims?*), in 1889 Ahmad "founded the Ahmadiyya Muslim Jama'at, under Divine guidance. Its main objective is to re-establish the original purity and beauty of Islam." According to that same pamphlet, Ahmadis believe that "in the 1880's, Hadhrat Mirza Ghulam Ahmad of Qadian declared himself to be the Promised Messiah and the Mahdi, under Divine commandment." In 1914 the community split into two factions, one based in the city of Qadian, and the other in Lahore. The Lahore branch of the community is active in the United States.

The Ahmadi community has a history of missionary activity outside of India, beginning with the establishment of the London Mission in 1914. Soon after this mission was established, Ahmadiyya missionaries began their work in North America. Mattias Gardell writes in his splendid 1996 book about the Nation of Islam, *In the Name of Elijah Muhammad: Louis Farrakhan and the Nation of Islam*: "since the 1921 establishment of their American headquarters in Chicago, the Ahmadiyya endeavored to obtain converts in the black community" (188). They published both a journal, *Review of Religions*, and a newspaper, *The Moslem Sunrise*, which were circulated in North America as part of Ahmadi missionary work, and met with some success, especially among African Americans. By the 1950s the Ahmadiyya were one of the few groups to attack publicly Elijah Muhammad and the Nation of Islam. As Gardell writes, "Their condemnation of the NOI was perhaps part of a twofold strategy to establish a profile as a genuine Islamic alternative among the African Americans and to enhance a mainstream Islamic status in the Muslim community" (188).

In the 1940s the Ahmadiyya community began to make a number of converts among African American Jazz musicians. By the 1950s the list included notables such as Art Blakey, Ahmad Jamal, McCoy Tyner, and Yusuf Lateef. Talib Dawood put together a seventeen-piece band composed entirely of American Muslim musicians, named The Messengers, an obvious reference to the many messengers and prophets that Muslims believe have been sent to earth. Later, Art Blakey would re-form a smaller version of the group as the Jazz Messengers. When you listen to Art Blakey and the Jazz Messengers, you are listening to American Muslim musicians perform an indigenous American musical form. These musicians also influenced other, non-Muslim musicians. So, for example, if one reads the great Dizzy Gillespie's 1979 autobiography, *To Be or Not to Bop*, one finds a number of references to Muslim Jazz musicians.

There were also rumors that the legendary John Coltrane had converted to Islam (he hadn't), and that the true title of his masterpiece, "A Love Supreme," was really "Allah Supreme" (it wasn't). However, Coltrane did record *Giant Steps* for, no surprise here, Atlantic Records in 1959. This was his most important piece of music to that date, and the first record to feature only his compositions. Four years earlier, Coltrane married his first wife, Naima, who was a convert to Islam. From her, he certainly became familiar with Islam, even if he never converted. He wrote the song "Naima" for her, which was part of *Giant Steps*. Their relationship was name-checked in the 1998 song "Astronomy (8th Light)" by the duo Blackstar, which consisted of American Muslim Hip Hop artists Talib Kweli and Mos Def: "I love rocking tracks like John Coltrane love Naima."

Also in the 1950s, as the Cold War developed, the U.S. government sent Jazz musicians out as ambassadors of American culture. African Americans were sent out to challenge Communist propaganda about American racism, but not surprisingly, they were often treated better abroad than at home, where there *was* institutionalized racism. Dizzy Gillespie and a young Quincy Jones were sent to Iran in 1956. This was just three years after the American government's coup to return the Shah of Iran to power after he had been ousted by the people of Iran. Dizzy's band was also sent to Syria, Lebanon, Turkey, and Pakistan. Two years later, Dave Brubeck was sent on a tour of Iraq. So there were interesting connections between American Jazz, officially sponsored by the U.S. government, and parts of the Muslim world. As discussed below, this program of "Jazz Diplomacy" would be revived in 2005 by the U.S. government as the Rhythm Road initiative, where this time Muslim Hip Hop artists were among the musicians sent out.

"BRING THE NOISE": RAP, HIP HOP, AND AMERICAN ISLAM

It is in Rap and Hip Hop that American Muslims have had their greatest impact on contemporary American music. I first became aware of this almost by accident, listening to a song by Public Enemy, one of the most influential and important Rap groups. In "Bring the Noise," from 1988's seminal *It Takes a Nation of Millions to Hold Us Back* (ranked number 48 on the *Rolling Stone* list of 500 greatest rock records, the highest position for a Hip Hop record),

Chuck D (born Carlton D. Ridenhour) had the following lines: "Cause a brother like me said, 'Well Farrakhan's
a prophet and I think you ought to listen to what he can
say to you, what you wanna do is follow for now.'" On
another track from that record, "Don't Believe the Hype,"
he rapped: "The follower of Farrakhan, don't tell me that
you understand until you hear the man."

There was Chuck D, who wasn't a Muslim, but who was
name-checking Louis Farrakhan, the leader of the Nation
of Islam. Some two decades later, I had the chance to meet
Chuck D in Leimert Plaza Park, the cultural heart of Black
Los Angeles. I asked him about those lines and why they
were in the songs, since Chuck wasn't a Muslim or a member of the Nation of Islam. Chuck just smiled and told me
that while he admired Minister Farrakhan, he also realized
that White kids bought Public Enemy records just as much
as Black kids did, and he chuckled to think of the reaction
of White parents to hearing their children sing lines of praise
about Minister Farrakhan. If the music of young people is
designed to help them rebel against their parents and authority figures, then Public Enemy (inducted into the Rock and
Roll Hall of Fame in 2013) were certainly doing their job.

Public Enemy gained even more publicity in 1989 with
their song "Fight the Power," which was prominently featured in the Spike Lee film *Do the Right Thing*. The full
version of the video that was released for the single featured the band in a march through Brooklyn, ending with
them performing against a backdrop that had two images.
The first was the Public Enemy logo, a man with a beret
(a Black Panthers homage) in the crosshairs of a gun sight.
The second was an image of Malcolm X, perhaps the most
famous member of the Nation of Islam. This was three
years before the release of Spike Lee's *Malcolm X* film in

1992 and showed the importance of Black nationalism, and Black Islam, in the work of Public Enemy.

In *In the Name of Elijah Muhammad*, Mattias Gardell wrote about the connections between African American Islam and Hip Hop: "The hip-hop movement's role in popularizing the message of black militant Islam cannot be overestimated. What reggae was to the expansion of the Rastafarian movement in the 1970s, so hip-hop is to the spread of black Islam in the 1980s and 1990s" (295).

"YOU ASK IF I'M A FIVE PERCENTER"

Alongside the Nation of Islam, the Five Percenters merit special attention here. Michael Muhammad Knight has done the best scholarly work on them. The Nation of the Five Percenters (also known as the Nation of Gods and Earths) has its roots in the Nation of Islam (NOI). Clarence 13X was a member of the NOI, who rose to a high rank in the Fruit of Islam, the paramilitary wing of the NOI. Clarence joined the NOI at Temple No. 7 in Harlem, where Malcolm X was the minister. He learned the Supreme Wisdom Lessons (also known as the Lost-Found Lessons) of the NOI, and broke with the NOI over a differing interpretation of them. One of the lessons talked about the original man being Black, and Clarence could not reconcile this with the fact that W. D. Fard, the founder of the NOI, and who was believed to be Allah in the flesh, was said to be only half-black, the son of a White woman. How, Clarence argued, could Allah be half-white if White people were the devil? (The ideology of the NOI described White people as literally devils, people who had the good, or blackness, bred out of them by an evil scientist, Mr. Yacoub.)

The name of the group came from the NOI's Supreme Wisdom Lessons, which taught that 85 percent of the world was uncivilized, 10 percent were the rich who enslaved that uncivilized majority, and 5 percent were the poor righteous teachers. The teachings of the Five Percenters were developed in their own lessons, which were taught orally from person to person. There was also a great deal of numerology and metaphor, known respectively as the Supreme Mathematics and the Supreme Alphabet. So different words and number combinations had hidden meanings and messages for Five Percenters. For example, the word "Allah" might be read by members as an acronym, "arm, leg, leg, arm, head," indicating their belief that as Black people, they were divine, Gods themselves. The word "Islam," to take another example, was usually translated in the Supreme Alphabet as "I Self Lord Am Master."

Felicia M. Miyakawa writes about the group in her book *Five Percenter Rap: God Hop's Music, Message, and Black Muslim Mission*:

> Rap is a perfect medium for spreading the Nation's doctrine. Rap not only captures the attention of an international audience, but also capitalizes on the Nation's emphasis on verbal ability. They quote and paraphrase Five Percenter lessons in lyrics; craft infectious grooves in order to capture the attention of their intended audience; make use of particular digital sound samples in order to create multiple levels of meaning; and give careful attention to album organization and packaging. Together these tools help Five Percenter musicians spread their message of redemption, a task eloquently outlined by Wise Intelligent of the rap group Poor Righteous Teachers: "Rap is [a] gardening tool. Get the brains right and exact so we can drop the seed. Drop the seed, fertilize it, and it's bound to grow to infinity." (37)

Many of the early Rap and Hip Hop performers, such as Big Daddy Kane and Rakim of Eric. B and Rakim, were influenced by Five Percenter ideology. While the Poor Righteous Teachers were an early Hip Hop group, the most influential Five Percenter group in Hip Hop (and certainly one of the most influential groups in Hip Hop) is the Wu-Tang Clan. On one reading, Wu-Tang refers to a mountain in China, where a Shaolin monk established his teachings. At a deeper level, using the Supreme Alphabet, the name instead is another acronym, indicating the group's origins in the Five Percenters: "Wisdom of the Universe and the Truth of Allah for the Nation of Gods." Both RZA (born Robert Diggs) and GZA (Gary Grice), along with many of the other members of the Wu-Tang Clan such as Ghostface Killa, Ol' Dirty Bastard, U-God, Raekwon, and Inspectah Deck are Muslim.

Another Muslim rapper is Ice Cube (born O'Shea Jackson), one of the key members of another seminal Rap group, N.W.A. If one saw the 2015 biographical film of them, *Straight Outta' Compton*, one would have seen a scene with Ice Cube in a Nation of Islam setting. In his 1992 song "When Will They Shoot?" Ice Cube rapped about his Muslim identity: "I met Farrakhan and had dinner / And you ask if I'm a Five-Percenter, well . . . / No, but I go where the brothers go / Down with Compton Mosque, Number 54." In 2008's "Gangsta Rap Made Me Do It," Cube rapped: "I never forgot Van Ness and Imperial / Look at my life, Ice Cube is a miracle / It could be you if you was this lyrical / It could be her if she was this spiritual / Cuz me and Allah go back like cronies / I don't got to be fake cause He is my homie." I must confess that hearing that song for the first time was the first time I heard a rapper speak of Allah as one of his homeboys, a response of sorts to the "Jesus is my Homeboy" and "Mary is my Homegirl" T-shirts and hats that one saw around Los Angeles at the end of the 1990s.

One could give more examples of the Islamic themes and allusions in the work of Ice Cube and Wu-Tang Clan, but this is not an exhaustive study of their music. Instead, for our purposes, it is important to note that two of the most important Rap and Hip Hop groups of all time have African American Muslim members, who often incorporate Muslim themes into their work. American Muslims, following the best American ideals, are important cultural producers.

THE SOUL OF WHITE FOLK

But it's not just African American Muslims who have influenced American Hip Hop. Everlast was born Erik Schrody in 1969 in California, where he developed a reputation as a graffiti artist and musician. Attracting the attention of rapper Ice-T, Everlast soon became a member of the Rhyme Syndicate, and toured with Ice-T. He later joined the Irish American Rap group, House of Pain, which became famous for the "Jump Around" single in 1992. Everlast came from a Catholic background, and had a tattoo of Sinn Féin, the Irish Republican political party, on his chest. However, through the African American artists in the worlds of Hip Hop and Rap described above, Everlast was exposed to the teachings of the Nation of Islam, and the Five Percenters. He then learned about orthodox Sunni Islam from Imam Warith Deen Mohammed and the Muslim American Society.

In 1997 Everlast became a convert to Islam. Of that conversion, he has said in an interview: "Islam made a lot of things make a lot of sense to me. It makes me look at life from a lot of different sides, and it's definitely one of the things that made me be honest enough with myself to sing and write some of the stuff about my life that I never would have let out before." The following year, he released a Hip Hop CD, *Whitey Ford Sings the Blues*, to commercial and critical success. His *Eat at Whitey's* CD released in 2000 has many explicit references to Islam. It ends with the track "Graves to Dig" that begins with the following lyrics: "They go one for the Prophet / Two for Islam / Three for the khutba from the Imam." The song continues with the following lyrics: "La ilaha ilala / Twelve rakahs short on a full day's prayer / Just hoping that the lord got some mercy to spare / One for the ummah / Two for the deen / Three for the angels, four for the alamin." Everlast continues to live and work in the Los Angeles area, yet another example of an influential American Muslim musician. In 2007, for example, he recorded the theme song to the television show *Saving Grace*, which starred Holly Hunter.

AMERICAN MUSLIM MUSIC

There are a number of other Muslim Hip Hop artists. Some are converts, like Busta Rhymes who came out (one notes the conscious borrowing of the term from another marginalized American community, namely the LGBTQ community) in 2007. Or Yasiin Bey (the former Mos Def), who made his conversion when he was nineteen years old. Others are born into Islam, performers like Talib Kweli, T-Pain, and Lupe Fiasco. In 2006 Lupe flipped the Kanye West single "Jesus Walks," releasing it as "Muhammad Walks." That's his most explicitly "Muslim" song about trying to get along, with lyrics such as: "Same God, different beliefs / Hijabs, Sunday clothes, yarmulke, kufi, same mission beneath / We all tryin' to get to where the sufferin' ends / In front of the Most High bein' judged for our sins / Can't front for the Most High, so the struggle continues." There is a lyricism and flow to Lupe's music that is quite extraordinary.

Of course, it's not only American Muslim men who are involved in Hip Hop. One of the important women, and one of the few to wear hijab when she performs, is Miss Undastood (born Tavasha Shannon). She was born in New York and started writing her work at age eleven while a student at the Al-Iman School in Queens (mentioned in chapter 4). The songs were a way for her to react against the strict Islamic norms of the school. However, as she grew, she changed her focus from writing songs about Thug life to writing what is often known as Conscious (for socially conscious) Hip Hop. The title of her first record, recorded in 2002, reflected this dichotomy, *Dunya or Deen* (which translates as "world or religion"). Her work reflects her identity as an American Muslim woman.

In 2009 Jennifer Taylor released her documentary *New Muslim Cool*. The film followed two Muslim brothers, Hamza and Sulaiman Perez. The Perez brothers are Puerto Rican converts to Islam, and also Hip Hop artists who founded a Muslim community in an inner-city part of Pittsburgh. This shows the multiethnicity of American Muslim Hip Hop, where one has Black, White, and Brown American Muslim artists. Of the importance of American Muslims to American Rap and Hip Hop, Hisham Aidi has written in an article for the *Middle East Report*:

> American hip-hop's relationship to Islam is thus inextricably linked to the century-long presence of Islam in the American inner city. References to Islam and Arabic terms are so legion that, for many young Americans weaned on hip-hop, rap videos and lyrics provide regular exposure to Islam. And Muslim youth abroad are keenly aware that, as popular wisdom has it, "Islam is hip-hop's official religion," and that Muslims like Busta Rhymes and Mos Def are some of rap's biggest players." (28)

Su'ad Abdul Khabeer is a professor at Purdue University, and is herself a brilliant spoken word artist. Her book

Muslim Cool: Race, Religion, and Hip Hop in the United States goes into much more detail about this "Muslim Cool," how American Muslims are understanding and living out the intertwining of their identities as Americans and as Muslims. Sometimes, this intertwining is used for political purposes.

In 2005 undersecretary of state for public diplomacy Karen Rhodes restarted the "Jazz Diplomacy" program as the Rhythm Road initiative for the George W. Bush administration. The program sent out American artists, including Muslim American artists such as Native Deen, to parts of the Muslim world. As described by Aidi,

> The tours have covered the broad arc of the Muslim world, with performances taking place in Senegal and Cote d'Ivoire, across North Africa, the Levant and Arabia, and extending to Mongolia, Pakistan and Indonesia. The artists stage performances and hold workshops; the hip-hop ambassadors who are Muslim talk to local media about being Muslim in America." (28)

That the American government has done this is a remarkable recognition of the worldwide appeal of the music that is performed by so many American Muslims.

There are also other forms of music performed by American Muslims, including country music. In 2006 Kareem Salama, an American Muslim who was born and raised in Oklahoma, released his first country record, *Generous Peace*. His 2011 record, *City of Lights*, has a song in praise of the Prophet Muhammad entitled "If I Could."

Muslims are also a presence in American Rock music. María Rosa Menocal published a groundbreaking book in 1987, *The Arabic Role in Medieval Literary History*. In that book, she talked about a possible derivation for the English word "troubadour" (in Provençal *trobar*) from the Arabic word *taraba*, meaning "to sing": "*Taraba* meant 'to sing' and sing poetry; *tarab* meant 'song,' and in the spoken Arabic of the Iberian peninsula it would have come to be pronounced *trob*; the formation of the Romance verb through addition of the *-ar* suffix would have been standard" (xi). So the tradition of troubadours, playing guitar and singing love poetry, which is a hallmark of medieval European society, also has deep roots in the Islamic world. In the contemporary world, one of the best modern troubadours is Richard Thompson, himself a British convert to Islam, who for the last three decades has been living in Los Angeles. That challenges our easy assumptions, that one of the best guitar players in the world is an American Muslim. Of spirituality in music, Richard has said, "Music is spiritual stuff, and even musicians who clearly worship money, or fame, or ego, cannot help but express a better part of themselves sometimes when performing, so great is the gift of music, and so connected to our higher selves. What we believe informs everything we do, and music is no exception."

In his magisterial book about the global appeal of Muslim music in youth culture, *Rebel Music*, Hisham Aidi wrote,

> An American Dream exists in Europe's Muslim ghettos and it's very much a black American one. For these young Europeans, America is home to African-American Islam, the oldest Muslim presence in the West, the Islam of Malcolm X and Muhammad Ali, an Islam that played a critical role in the civil rights movement and in making America more at ease with diversity than Europe. (xvi)

Aidi's words show the importance and influence of American Muslim music—and American Muslim musicians—not just in America, but around the world.

3
The Greatest

Sports

THE GREATEST BASKETBALL PLAYER IN THE WORLD

During the 2015–2016 NBA season, much was made of the retirement of Los Angeles Lakers shooting guard Kobe Bryant. Many commentators argued his place among the top basketball players of all time, and more than a few suggested that he was the greatest Los Angeles Laker. As a Lakers fan for some four decades, Kobe, great as he was and with no disrespect to him, doesn't make my top *five* list of greatest Lakers, let alone greatest basketball players of all time. (For anyone interested, my top five Los Angeles Lakers in order would be Kareem Abdul-Jabbar, Earvin "Magic" Johnson, Jerry West, Wilt Chamberlain, and Shaquille O'Neal. George Mikan gets an honorary mention, but he played when the team was in Minneapolis, long before it moved to Los Angeles.) The greatest basketball coach ever, the late John R. Wooden, thought that one of his college players at UCLA was the greatest basketball player ever. That was yet another American Muslim, Kareem Abdul-Jabbar. When comparing his statistics with anyone else who played high school, college, and professional basketball, I cannot understand why more people don't agree with Coach Wooden. In our haste to anoint Steph Curry, LeBron James, or Michael Jordan as the best ever (again, with no disrespect to any of them), we forget about Kareem. Perhaps, as discussed below, his being an African American Muslim is connected to our amnesia.

Kareem was born Ferdinand Lewis Alcindor Jr. in New York City in 1947. He grew up Roman Catholic, and attended a Catholic school, Power Memorial Academy in the city, where his high school team lost two games and won one high school national championship.

Heavily recruited for college, he chose the University of California, Los Angeles (UCLA), whose coach, John R. Wooden, had won his first national championship for UCLA in 1964. Kareem came to UCLA in 1966 but was unable to play that year due to a quaint rule that prohibited freshmen from competing in intercollegiate athletics. Apparently, people at that time thought that education was important for those enrolled in a university, and that freshmen athletes needed a year to adjust to the demands of campus life. And yes, full disclosure, I am one of those professors who believe that student athletes should be students first and athletes second.

In his three years of eligibility at UCLA, Kareem was three-time player of the year, three-time finals MVP and three-time NCAA champion. In other words, he had three perfect seasons while he earned his degree. He lost the same number of games, two, at UCLA, that he did in high school. We think of Kareem with the iconic sky-hook, but he could also throw down the thunder. How many of us remember that, after his first season at UCLA in 1967, the NCAA outlawed dunking? That wasn't solely because of Kareem, to be sure, but in the racially charged atmosphere of the late 1960s, between the assassinations of Malcolm X and Martin Luther King Jr., it must surely have been intimidating to some to see large Black men slam the ball home with authority. Michael Jordan was a phenomenal dunker (almost as good as Clyde Drexler), but no one ever outlawed the dunk because of him.

It was at UCLA that Kareem became interested in Islam, reading *The Autobiography of Malcolm X* as a freshman. In that first year at UCLA, he met Muhammad Ali, who had joined the Nation of Islam a few years earlier. Later, in Harlem, Ali took Kareem to meet Louis Farrakhan. Kareem did not join the NOI, writing in a June 6, 2016, remembrance of Ali for *Time* magazine that "my burgeoning involvement with Islam was strictly a spiritual quest, while the Nation of Islam seemed more of a political organization. I wanted to keep my pursuit of social justice separate from my pursuit of religious fulfillment."

He converted in 1971, taking on the new name of Kareem Abdul-Jabbar. In his own writings, he has described that conversion, and the issues that arose with his mentor, Hamaas Abdul Khaalis. Abdul Khaalis had joined the NOI, but left to set up his own Sunni Muslim organization, the Hanafi Movement (named for one of the key founding jurists of Islamic law). He wrote a letter in 1972 criticizing the NOI, and the following year gunmen broke into the home that Kareem had purchased for Abdul Khaalis and killed his family members.

In March of 1977, twelve armed followers of Abdul Khaalis took over three buildings in D.C., including the Islamic Center of Washington that had been built after the death of Munir Ertegun. They held hostages for several days, and a reporter, Maurice Williams, was killed. The key people in the hostage negotiations were three Muslim ambassadors, Ashraf Ghorbal from Egypt, Ardeshir Zahedi from Iran, and Sahabzada Yaqub-Khan from Pakistan. Through using the Qur'an and Islamic teachings on mercy and compassion, they persuaded the hostage takers to surrender. Kareem, of course, was distraught at what Abdul Khaalis and his gunmen had done.

At the end of 1977, Joni Mitchell released her ninth studio record, *Don Juan's Reckless Daughter*, whose third side opened with the song "Otis and Marlena," with its reference to the hostage situation: "They've come for sun and fun / While Muslims stick up Washington." This was not Joni's first reference to Islam, as the year before she had released *Hejira*, named for the migration of the Prophet Muhammad from Mecca to Medina. These are other small examples of the influence of Islam on American cultural production, how Muslim tropes end up in the American mainstream.

SPIRITUAL CONNECTIONS

For Kareem, Islam represented a religious tradition that was familiar to him. Growing up Catholic, Kareem was exposed to stories of the Bible, and particularly to the figures of Mary and Jesus from the New Testament. In Islam, he encountered those same biblical stories and characters. And both Mary and Jesus also play prominent roles in the Qur'an.

The Qur'an mentions Mary and Jesus, as well as other figures from the New Testament such as John the Baptist and Zechariah. In fact, Mary is mentioned more by name in the Qur'an (34 times) than she is in the New Testament (19 times). The story of the virgin birth of Jesus is mentioned in the Qur'an. The Qur'an speaks about the fact that Mary was criticized by some in her community, who could not accept the virgin birth. Mary asks Jesus to speak on his own behalf, and he does so, in what is a lovely, succinct account of Islamic Christology:

> Mary pointed to the child then; but they said, "How shall we speak to one who is still in the cradle, a little child?" Jesus said, "Lo, I am God's servant; God has given me the book and made me a prophet. God has made me blessed, wherever I may be; and God has enjoined me to pray and to give alms so long as I live, and likewise to cherish my mother; God has not made me arrogant or unprosperous. Peace be upon me the day I was born, and the day I die, and the day I am raised up alive." (Qur'an 19:30-35)

Jesus is an important figure for Muslims. He is mentioned in fifteen chapters and ninety-three verses of the Qur'an. In the Qur'an, Jesus is described by many names: by his proper name, Jesus; as "Son of Mary," twenty-three times in the Qur'an (it is interesting to note that Jesus is only referred to by this title once in the New Testament, in Mark 6:3); and as Servant of God; Prophet; Messenger; Word; Spirit; Sign; Parable or Example; Witness; A Mercy; Eminent; Brought near to God; Upright; Blessed.

There are also a number of miracles associated with Jesus: As described above, he speaks from the cradle as an infant. He creates birds from clay, and they come to life and fly away (a parallel with the noncanonical *Infancy Gospel of Thomas*). He heals the blind and the lepers. He raises the dead. He feeds his followers with a table from heaven.

Eleven times in the Qur'an, Jesus is referred to as "Messiah." But this simply means "the anointed one," a direct parallel with the usage in Hebrew. Although "Messiah" is translated into Greek as "Christ," and assumes divine significance for Christians, it is important to point out the differences between Christian and Muslim usages of that term. The Qur'an expresses the Muslim understanding of Jesus in the following verse: "The Messiah, Jesus son of Mary, was only the messenger of God, and God's word that God committed to Mary, and a spirit from God" (Qur'an 4:169).

So with Islam, Kareem, as with most Christians, was in familiar religious territory. He had the Jesus and Mary that he knew from his Catholic childhood. He also knew his history, described in the previous chapter: that some slaves brought over from West Africa were Muslim. So it wasn't so much a "conversion" to Islam, as it was a reversion to the ways of his ancestors.

For many (but not Kareem) there was also the political statement to be made, the connections between Christianity, slavery, and racism. To convert to Islam was also a way for an African American to renounce the racism and discrimination of American Christianity. It is instructive, here, to remember that when Dr. Martin Luther King Jr. wrote his magisterial "Letter from Birmingham City Jail," it was addressed not generically to White people, but to a specific group of eight White Christian clergy from Alabama, who in their own "A Call for Unity" saw his civil disobedience as both un-Christian and un-American. For many, to become a Muslim in the 1960s was to make a very powerful statement about the racism in White Christian America.

There is also an older connection here between athletics and civil rights. It was African American athletes who were the trailblazers for full inclusion. So one thinks of Jack Johnson becoming the first African American heavyweight champion in 1908, Jesse Owens winning four gold medals at the Berlin Olympics in 1936, or Joe Louis knocking out Max Schmeling in 1938. A decade later, in 1947, Jackie Robinson became the first modern player to break the color line in Major League Baseball. So it was American athletes, African American athletes, who helped us to realize another

American ideal of equality. Kareem continued that tradition as an African American Muslim athlete.

KAREEM REDUX: THE LION IN WINTER

Following his conversion, Kareem excelled in the pros just as much as he did in college and high school. Six NBA championships, six NBA MVP awards, a nineteen-time all-star, and the NBA's all-time leading scorer. Couple that with his three NCAA championships, and I don't know how you can make the case for anyone else as the greatest basketball player of all time.

But Kareem is not your typical professional athlete. He's quiet and soft-spoken, not one to seek the media spotlight. He's also an accomplished writer. Besides his two volumes of autobiography, he's also published a half-dozen nonfiction books, and recently has been doing a column on religion for *Time* magazine. Kareem came from the generation that grew up with the civil rights movement in the 1960s, those who spoke out against injustice. Those who stood up at great risk to themselves. Gary Smith wrote one of his magisterial columns for *Sports Illustrated* about this, the athletes who spoke out in the 1960s and 1970s, and the later ones who didn't. Modern athletes, to take Michael Jordan or Eldrick "Tiger" Woods as the most obvious examples, have learned not to make a fuss, to endorse the status quo, and take the millions (and millions) of dollars that come with their silence.

Kareem was never a house negro (to use the distinction that Malcolm X made famous between a house negro who did his master's bidding—and so was fed scraps from his master's table in reward—and a field negro who was tasked with much harsher work for his insolence to his master). As a result, the greatest basketball player *ever* can't get a job coaching in the NBA. Instead, Luke Walton (and I remind the reader, that's *Luke* Walton, Bill's son, not Bill Walton, the NBA legend) is now the coach of my beloved Lakers, and countless White college coaches with losing records get called up to try their hands in the NBA.

One can begin to look at Kareem's activism in 1968, after his junior season at UCLA, when he had won an NCAA championship and been named player of the year. Not surprisingly, he was invited to try out for the U.S. men's basketball team at the upcoming Olympics in Mexico City (these were the days, long before the "dream team" of Barcelona in 1992, when professionals were not allowed to compete in the Olympics). However, the year before, the Olympic Project for Human Rights had been formed under the leadership of Berkeley sociologist Harry Edwards. Like many, Edwards was concerned about the state of civil rights in our country, and the OPHR called for a boycott of the Olympics by African American athletes. Almost a decade earlier, Muhammad Ali had won the light heavyweight gold medal at the Rome Olympics, only to face racism and discrimination in his hometown of Louisville. Kareem was supportive of both Edwards and the OPHR, even though in the end his decision to stay at home and not to participate in the tryouts for the Olympic team was due to his summer job commitment in New York City. He was interviewed by Joe Garagiola on the *Today* show, and voiced his frustrations, saying that sometimes the United States felt like it wasn't his country. Garagiola, reflecting the temper of the times, suggested that perhaps Kareem should move, an extraordinary thing to say to a twenty-year-old American college student. The boycott didn't take place, but Tommie Smith and John Carlos protested at the medal ceremony for the two hundred meters, heads bowed, black-gloved fists in the air.

Of course, Kareem is not only openly Black, he's also openly Muslim. He's written about the difficulties of being an American Muslim in the post-9/11 world. And while there have been numerous Muslim basketball players, both American converts such as Jamaal Wilkes, or foreign-born players such as hall of famer Hakeem "the Dream" Olajuwon, perhaps the NBA isn't ready for a Muslim head coach, even if said head coach is the greatest ever at the game.

BEFORE STEPH CURRY, THERE WAS MAHMOUD ABDUL-RAUF

The issues that the NBA has with Muslim Americans go back to before the 9/11 attacks. How many of us remember the name Mahmoud Abdul-Rauf, and the controversy surrounding his decision not to stand for the national anthem before one game in 1996? Abdul-Rauf was born Chris Jackson, in Gulfport, Mississippi. He excelled as a point guard, and joined the Louisiana State University Tigers in 1988. I became aware of him not because of his phenomenal quickness (at six feet tall, one had to be quick to play major college basketball), but because of his Tourette's syndrome. Tourette's is a neuropsychiatric inherited disease, which often manifests itself in tics and muscle spasms that result in involuntary jerks. To have the body control required of an All-American point guard, while at the same time dealing with the tics and spasms of Tourette's, made Chris Jackson's story extraordinary.

In his freshman season, Jackson was chosen as player of the year in the South East Conference. He was the first SEC freshman to be so honored. Chris repeated as SEC player of the year (as well as repeating as an All-American) in his sophomore season, when he was joined on the LSU team by an even more heavily recruited player, center Shaquille O'Neal. That's when people often start remembering Chris. If you watched Shaq run the floor for those LSU Tigers, you often saw Chris passing him the ball, or stepping outside to shoot when defenses doubled down on Shaq. And it was Chris, not Shaq, who was SEC player of the year. In the aftermath of Stephen Curry's spectacular back-to-back seasons as NBA MVP in 2015 and 2016, some veterans, like Phil Jackson, have remembered Chris Jackson, and how he was Steph Curry before Steph was Steph Curry.

Coming from a single-parent family of modest means in Gulfport, Chris left LSU after his sophomore season and declared for the NBA draft in order to provide for his family. He was drafted in the first round by the Denver Nuggets, the third player chosen after Derrick Coleman and Gary Payton. It was in Denver that Chris converted to Islam. After a visit to the mosque in Denver, Chris was given a Qur'an. He read that, and also read *The Autobiography of Malcolm X*. He converted in 1991 and later changed his name to Mahmoud Abdul-Rauf.

In 1996 he was at the center of controversy when he refused to stand for the national anthem before a Nuggets home game. In a lovely documentary directed by anthropologist Zareena Grewal, *By the Dawn's Early Light: Chris Jackson's Journey to Islam*, Abdul-Rauf spoke about the emphasis on justice that he found in the Qur'an. He also spoke about his understanding of the oneness of God as expressed in the statement of faith: "I bear witness that there is no god but God." For him that meant that no one was worthy of worship but God, and standing for the anthem elevated the nation to an equal status with God. The NBA suspended him for one game. Interestingly, the NBA never took action on the players who were Jehovah's Witnesses who did not stand for the anthem out of respect for their identical religious beliefs that standing for a flag and an anthem could be construed as idolatry.

Abdul-Rauf was able to speak with Muslim leaders, as well as Muslim basketball players such as Hakeem Olajuwon and Kareem Abdul-Jabbar, and rethink his position. He decided to stand, but to bow his head and offer a short prayer instead. That summer, he was traded by the Denver Nuggets to the Sacramento Kings. He was then traded to a Canadian team, the Memphis Grizzlies. A few years after the controversy, one of the NBA's best players, someone who was averaging a point per minute played, was out of the league and playing overseas in Europe and Asia. There was a sense of déjà vu in the way that Abdul-Rauf was treated over his religious beliefs. He knew racism and discrimination as a Black man in Mississippi, and he faced religious discrimination when he took a principled stand as an American Muslim.

MUSLIMS IN THE NBA

While there are many other American Muslims who have played in the NBA, Hakeem Olajuwon is important to mention here. He came to America the way many Muslims do, as a university student. Hakeem went from his home in Lagos, Nigeria, to Houston, to play college basketball at the University of Houston. There, he became the first player from a losing team to be named the NCAA Tournament Most Outstanding Player. Hakeem continued his success in the NBA, being drafted first overall by the Houston Rockets. Hakeem led the team to two NBA titles, and in 1994 he became the first (and only) player to win the NBA MVP, Defensive Player of the Year, and Finals MVP awards all in the same year. In 1996 he helped our country win a second straight gold medal at the Atlanta Olympics. In 2008 Hakeem was inducted into the Naismith Memorial Basketball Hall of Fame.

Hakeem was also born into a Muslim family, and his faith was important to him, including during his playing days. He was observant, and would fast during the month of Ramadan, even when that conflicted with his NBA schedule. That's something that Muslim athletes have to consider, if they will play or practice while they are fasting. Since the fast is a total fast, including not drinking any water, it can be a hardship for a professional athlete. In retirement, Hakeem has deepened his understanding of his faith, spending part of his time each year studying Islam.

There are rumors that another NBA great, Shaquille O'Neal, is also a Muslim. That would make three American Muslims in the Hall of Fame. The man who raised Shaquille, his stepfather Phillip Harrison, is a Muslim. While others have said that Shaq is a Muslim, he himself has been ambiguous about his own religious beliefs.

THE GREATEST OF ALL TIME: AN AMERICAN MUSLIM

If we want to discuss American Muslim athletes who were outspoken about their faith, and suffered hardship because of their Muslim beliefs, we need to go back to the Greatest of All Time, Muhammad Ali. Long before his conversion to Islam, the young Cassius Clay knew controversy with the racism in his hometown of Louisville in the 1950s and 1960s. In 1960 Clay represented our country at the Rome Olympics, winning the boxing light heavyweight gold medal. Upon his return home, he was refused service in a local diner. Think of that for a minute, a young man who had won six state Golden Gloves titles, two national

Golden Gloves titles, and an Olympic gold medal, but unfortunately was the wrong color to get something to eat in his hometown. However, Ali continued to love his hometown. In 2005 the Muhammad Ali Center was opened in Louisville. At his funeral celebration on June 10, 2016, the city showed its love for him with a procession through the city's streets.

Clay turned professional in 1960 and became known as much for his verbal skills as for his boxing skills. A 2006 book, *Ali Rap*, collected many of his sayings in making the argument that he was the originator of Rap. He wasn't, but the poetry that he and his cornerman Drew Bundini Brown created has had lasting significance in American culture.

In 1964 the twenty-two-year-old Clay, by his own admission, "shook up the world" in his six-round defeat of Sonny Liston, becoming the world heavyweight boxing champion. A few years earlier, Clay had gone to Nation of Islam meetings. There, he met Malcolm X, who as a friend and advisor was part of Clay's entourage for the Liston fight. Clay made his conversion public after the fight, and was renamed by Elijah Muhammad as Muhammad Ali. When Malcolm X left the Nation of Islam because of his issues with Elijah Muhammad, Ali broke with his old friend.

Ali could be cruel, with an arrogance to match his unmatchable skill. He prolonged several fights: one with Floyd Patterson, and another with Ernie Terrell. In this latter fight, when Terrell would not call Ali by his new name, he kept punishing him for the full fifteen rounds of a fight he could have ended much sooner, repeatedly asking Terrell, "What's my name?" However, Ali also had a conscience. When he was reclassified as eligible for induction into the draft for the Vietnam War, Ali refused on the grounds of his new Muslim religious beliefs. Famously, he said that "war is against the teachings of the Holy Koran. I'm not trying to dodge the draft. We are not supposed to take part in no wars unless declared by Allah or the Messenger [Elijah Muhammad]. We don't take part in Christian wars or wars of any unbelievers." Even more famously, reflecting on the racism he had experienced in America, Ali said, "I ain't got no quarrel with them Viet Cong—no Viet Cong ever called me Ni**er." This conscientious objector status *was* rooted in the teachings of the Nation of Islam, and Elijah Muhammad had been jailed for his refusal to enter the draft in World War II.

On April 28, 1967, Ali refused induction into the draft. He was arrested, and his boxing titles were stripped from him. Ali never went to prison, but he couldn't box for over three years. Think about that for a minute. There was Ali, at age twenty-five at the height of his athletic prowess ("Like a rock / I was something to see," as Bob Seger would sing in 1986 of his own salad days), three years into his undefeated reign as world heavyweight champion. And Ali might not have faced danger in Vietnam, so it wasn't about any kind of cowardice. Almost a decade earlier, Elvis Presley had been inducted into the U.S. Army. Elvis refused any kind of privileges with special services, but with no war being waged at that time, he also didn't have to serve on the front line. Elvis was instead assigned to a U.S. Army base in West Germany. The Champ most likely wouldn't have been put on the front lines. He would be a celebrity, giving exhibitions for the troops to boost morale. But for him, as a Muslim, as a Black Muslim, the Vietnam War was wrong. In 1967 that was not the popular stance that it is today, and Ali paid dearly, unable to make a living at the trade for which he was eminently qualified, at the peak of his talents.

Ali's case went to the U.S. Supreme Court, which ruled unanimously on June 28, 1971, to overturn his conviction. The Court did this on a technicality, since the appeal court had never given a reason for why Ali was denied conscientious objector status. But Ali was free, and able to resume his work.

His later boxing history is well known to sports fans: the loss to Joe Frazier in 1971 (his first professional loss), the loss to Ken Norton in 1973 (fighting the full twelve rounds despite a jaw broken by Norton), the rematch win with Frazier in 1974, the regaining of his heavyweight title later that year against Foreman, the conclusion of the Holy Trinity (fights of the type between Frazier and Ali must be

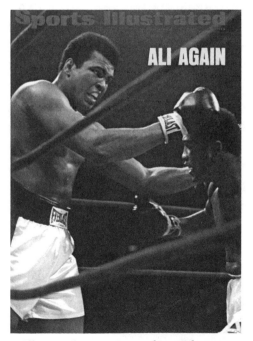

Sports Illustrated *Cover Image from February 4, 1974*

given their proper religious title, and not the more mundane sports title of "trilogy") with his second win against Frazier (what Ali famously called "the closest thing to dying that I know"), becoming the first three-time heavyweight champion in his rematch with Leon Spinks in 1978, and the brutal beat down at the hands of Larry Holmes in 1980 that effectively ended Ali's career as a boxer.

But there he was, an American Muslim who changed America. In 1975 he followed Warith Deen Mohammed, who took his father's Nation of Islam into Sunni orthodoxy. He became a proselytizer for Islam, giving out pamphlets inviting others to Islam, autographed so that he knew they would be kept by those who received them. And as people began to see what Ali had done in the 1960s, he became a hero not just for his athletic prowess, but for his work on civil rights. Who can forget in 1996, when the opening ceremonies were held for the Olympics in Atlanta? There was Janet Evans, one of the most decorated American swimmers, the last athlete to hold the torch, who we all thought would light the Olympic cauldron. And there she was, passing the torch to Ali, who held the torch aloft in his right hand, but whose left hand was shaking with Parkinson's syndrome. In the hush of the crowd, it was Ali who would light the cauldron, something that he would repeat at the Winter Olympics in Salt Lake City in 2002. American Muslims, as President Obama reminded us, "have lit the Olympic Torch."

Ali's funeral on June 10, 2016, showed the outpouring of love and support for him. This was a beloved American hero returning home, a beloved American Muslim. When we think of Muslims in this country, let us think of Ali, and continue to honor his life and work.

MUSLIM BOXERS

Ali is the most famous American Muslim boxer, but he's not the only one. Mike Tyson also held the heavyweight championship, the youngest ever to hold such a title. Tyson is included in the conversation about the best heavyweight boxers, and the greatest punchers. In 1986 I saw Tyson brutalize Marvis Frazier (Joe's son) with a knockout that took less than thrity seconds. However, Tyson also spent three years, from 1992 to 1995, in a prison in Indiana following his rape conviction. That prison, Plainfield Correctional Facility, was located in Plainfield, the headquarters of the Islamic Society of North America. It was there that Tyson made his conversion to Islam. Tyson is still a Muslim, and often speaks about his own practice of Islam. He's not perfect, goodness knows, but he does what he can to live out his faith as best as he can. How many of us, after all, can claim to live up to the ideals of our own religious traditions.

In addition to his boxing legacy, Tyson has also become known for his television and movie work. And in the second act of his American life, he has achieved recognition for his one-man show, "Mike Tyson: Undisputed Truth." In that show, he speaks openly and honestly about his life and times. Clearly, Mike Tyson has had an impact, as an American Muslim, on American culture, not just on American sport.

To take only one more example, another boxer who converted to Islam in prison is Bernard Hopkins. Past the age of fifty, Hopkins astonishingly continues as a professional boxer. He came to fame with a decade-long run as a middleweight champion. Now, he fights as a light heavyweight. As a young man, Hopkins was sentenced to prison, finding his way out through both boxing and Islam. That's important to remember, that a conversion to Islam means that sometimes people can give up past bad habits.

AMERICAN MUSLIMS AND AMERICAN SPORT

American Muslims have influenced other American sports, including at the Olympics. One thinks of Ibtihaj Muhammad, a member of the U.S. Fencing Team. At the 2016 Olympics, she became the first American woman to compete in hijab. Born into a Muslim family, she has traveled to learn about her own faith. As an American Muslim woman, she is also part of the U.S. Department of State's Empowering Women and Girls Through Sports Initiative.

There have also been American Muslims who played in the National Football League. One name that usually comes to mind is that of Ahmad Rashad, the wide receiver for the Minnesota Vikings, who was perhaps the most famous Muslim convert in the NFL. But there are many other American Muslims who followed in Rashad's footsteps. One thinks of Muhammad Wilkerson, a defensive end for the New York Jets. Or of the Abdullah brothers, Husain and Hamza, both safeties in the NFL. The brothers are observant, and both took the 2012 season off to make the pilgrimage to Mecca. Both fast during the month of Ramadan, and yet still compete and practice with their teams. In 2014 Husain Abdullah gained some notoriety when he returned an interception for a touchdown, and then prostrated himself in the way that he would for Islamic prayer, giving thanks to God. For this, he was given an unsportsmanlike conduct penalty. The NFL later apologized for this, and said he shouldn't have been penalized, as Christian athletes who kneel in Christian prayer are not penalized.

Aqib Talib, a cornerback for the Denver Broncos, is one of the best defensive players in the NFL. In 2016 he was part of the Denver team that won Super Bowl 50. So an American Muslim has helped his team win a Super Bowl.

Another American Muslim, Shahid Khan, actually *owns* an NFL team. In 2011 Khan purchased the Jacksonville Jaguars. Khan is another American Muslim success story. He came to the United States from Pakistan in 1967 to study engineering at the University of Illinois at Urbana-Champaign. While at school he worked for an automotive manufacturing company, which he later bought and turned into a multibillion-dollar business. In 1991 he became a U.S. citizen. Khan has lived out the ultimate American ideal of success, becoming a billionaire through his hard work, and not through inheriting family wealth.

There are other American Muslim athletes that one could list here, but the point is not to compile an exhaustive list. The point is to state that the contributions that American Muslims have made to American sport have been invaluable. The greatest boxer ever, Muhammad Ali, was an American Muslim. The greatest basketball player ever, Kareem Abdul-Jabbar, is an American Muslim. They are the two greatest, but there are countless others. They sometimes face hardship because of their faith, such as women who wear hijab while competing, who may need to get special permission to do so. They may face discrimination for standing up for their Muslim beliefs. They may need to exempt themselves from competition to perform the prescribed daily prayers, monthly fast, or annual pilgrimage. But they persevere, as American Muslims, in their contributions to American life.

4

Muslims on the American Landscape
Culture

ISLAM IN THE CULTURAL HISTORY OF AMERICA

The University of Southern California (USC) has one of the finest architecture schools in the country. My Toronto homeboy, Frank Gehry, perhaps the world's greatest living architect, is one of its graduates. A decade ago, a Canadian Muslim friend was accepted there to study architecture. He knew that there was a significant Muslim student population at USC, and that they had a mosque close to the campus. That is Masjid Omar Ibn Al-Khattab, which was built in 1994. On the first Friday that he was on the USC campus, the week before classes started, my friend crossed Jefferson Boulevard to go to the mosque for the congregational prayer. He thought that this would be a great chance to connect with the Muslim community at USC. However, when my friend got to the mosque, he was puzzled that the doors were locked, and that there were very few people around. Trying to open one of the doors, he attracted the attention of a security guard. The guard asked him what he was doing. My friend responded that he was trying to get into the mosque for the Friday afternoon prayer. The guard smiled and told my friend that there was no Friday prayer there, since the structure wasn't a mosque. It was the Shrine Auditorium. The mosque *was* a couple of blocks away, but it was across the USC campus from Vermont Avenue, not Jefferson Boulevard.

The Shrine Auditorium

That day, my friend got an introduction to architecture in America that is inspired by Islam. The Shrine Auditorium was opened in 1926, one of many such auditoriums built around the country by the Shriners. It is perhaps the most famous Shriner landmark, key to the cultural history of America, a space that has hosted both the Academy Awards and the Grammy Awards. Gulzar Haider, the most famous North American Muslim architect, tells his own story about Shriner architecture in his chapter in the edited volume *Making Muslim Space in North America and Europe*. In 1960 Haider was at the University of Pittsburgh on a Fulbright-Hays scholarship. His host family took him to the nearby Syria Mosque, another auditorium built by the Shriners in a Moorish style (complete with the same Arabic calligraphy that is found on the Alhambra in Granada).

The Shriners, of course, are not Muslim, but a Masonic group. Their buildings represent a fascination with the "Orient" that America has had for a century. These days, we think of the "Orient" as being the Far East, countries like China, Korea, and Japan. But at the beginning of the twentieth century, the "Orient" meant the Near East. My mentor, Wilfred Cantwell Smith, completed his degree at the University of Toronto in 1938 in what was then known as Oriental languages, meaning he studied Arabic and Hebrew, as well as other ancient Semitic languages. In Los Angeles, one finds interesting connections between the "Orient" and the early days of the motion picture industry in Southern California.

In 1907 Francis Boggs came to Los Angeles to shoot a few scenes to complete *The Count of Monte Cristo*. The following year, he shot the first film on location in Los Angeles, *In the Power of the Sultan*, starring Hobart Bosworth. No copy of that film survives, but it's intriguing to remember that the first film shot in Los Angeles was also about the Orient. The portrayals weren't always positive (a review of *In the Power of the Sultan* mentions "the despised Sultan," as well as another villainous Turk, one Osman Bey). The malevolent Hollywood sheikh was a stock character in early American films, one who was lecherous and cruel. This is best exemplified in the 1921 film *The Sheikh*, where Rudolf Valentino's title character, Sheikh Ahmed, boasts that "when an Arab sees a woman he wants, he takes her." Jack Shaheen has done the key work here: his book *Reel Bad Arabs* looks at the way that Arabs, and Muslims, have been vilified in Hollywood films. In 1922 Howard Carter opened the tomb of King Tutankhamun in Egypt and the fascination with the Orient only increased in America.

In 1926 the city of Opa-locka was founded in Miami-Dade County, Florida. It was an entire city built on the

Moorish revival theme of Shriner architecture, with some 105 original buildings. Unfortunately, many of them were damaged later that year by a hurricane, and had to be rebuilt between 1926 and 1928. Today, twenty of them are on the National Register of Historic Places, and the old city hall, with its multiple pink domes, has been turned into an artistic and cultural center.

To take a more well-known example of this American fascination with the Orient, in 1913 the R. J. Reynolds tobacco company introduced Camel cigarettes, modeled on Egyptian cigarettes and using Turkish tobacco and Turkish paper. The symbols are quite clear: the camel, the palm trees, and the pyramid, stock images of the Arab world.

Camel Cigarettes Logo

Or to take a more recent example of a faux Islamic building that plays on this fascination with the Orient, consider a landmark Atlantic City casino, the Trump Taj Mahal. It was built in 1990, at the time one of the largest casinos in the world. It was such a spectacle that one of my closest college friends chose it as the location for his bachelor party in 1992. The first and only time I visited the casino was on that occasion. Some twenty-five years later, it's interesting to consider the attitude toward Muslims of the man whose name is on the building. Back then, Mr. Trump seemed to have no problem with Muslims, and named his signature casino after one of the most important Muslim buildings in the world, the Taj Mahal. The Taj Mahal is not a mosque, of course, but a mausoleum. But it is also one of the most beautiful buildings in the world. So we here in America have long had a fascination with and admiration of Islamic architecture.

The Taj Mahal Casino

AMERICAN MOSQUES

As outlined in the first chapter, the first mosque in America was built by Albanians in Maine in 1915. Since then, there have been a number of American mosques that have been built. Gulzar Haider designed one of the most impressive ones, the mosque for the Islamic Society of North America in Plainfield, Indiana. Haider went to school at the University of Illinois at Urbana-Champaign. This was the same school (discussed below) that had earlier educated the great structural engineer, Fazlur Rahman Khan. It was at the Urbana-Champaign campus, while Haider was a student there, that the MSA formed.

In 1979 Haider was asked to design the mosque for the organization that would become ISNA, and he completed it in 1982. It's a fascinating building, with no dome visible from the outside, but three separate domes internal to the building. It's a building that doesn't look out of place in the Indiana suburb where it is located—just another commercial building composed of rectangles. From the inside, however, it is quite stunning. There was a deliberate decision by Haider not to do the typical domes and minarets that had been associated with the Moorish revival style described above. Instead, he wanted to, in his words, "veil this mosque," playing with the tension in Islam between God being the Manifest as well as the Hidden. These are two of the ninety-nine Most Beautiful Names of God.

If one begins to look, one sees other mosques across this country as well. A 2011 study of American mosques counted some 2,106. The most mosques were to be found in New York (257), California (246), and Texas (166). At one end of the country, to take only one very public example, on the Van Wyck Expressway, on the drive from JFK Airport into Manhattan, one sees the Imam Al-Khoei Foundation and Mosque. This was a foundation established in 1989 by one of the most important Shi'a leaders in the world, Ayatollah Seyyid Abulqasim Al-Khoei, who lived and taught in Najaf, Iraq. The foundation has a school, Al-Iman, which was established a year later. It is one of the major Shi'a institutions in New York City, and as much a part of the landscape of its Jamaica, Queens neighborhood as the adjacent Jamaica Hospital Medical Center.

On the Upper East Side of Manhattan, one finds the Islamic Cultural Center of New York, a large and impressive mosque that was opened in 1991. Prior to that, worship for this congregation took place on the Upper West Side, in a townhouse at Riverside Drive and 72nd Street. That small mosque is still in use, and I have prayed in it several times on trips to my beloved Upper West Side.

New York City, the metropolitan area with the most mosques (192), has a long history of mosques. In 1893 Alexander Russell Webb established a small prayer space in Manhattan alongside his publishing house. Perhaps the first mosque in the city was a public hall on Powers Street in Brooklyn, purchased in 1928 by Tatar immigrants from the Baltic and converted into a mosque. Jerrilynn Dodds and Edward Grazda published a book in 2002, *New York Masjid: The Mosques of New York City*, which described some of the mosques in the city. The book was planned after the attacks on the World Trade Center in 1993 and the accusations that terrorists used the mosques of New York City to plot out their atrocities. The book was finished a month before the attacks of 9/11 that brought down the World Trade Center, and revised as a result. It provides extraordinary photographs to document the rich architectural presence of mosques in New York City.

There have been controversies around the building of American mosques before the 9/11 attacks. In 1997 I moved to Northridge in the San Fernando Valley to begin teaching at California State University, Northridge. I knew that there was a large new mosque in the adjacent neighborhood of Granada Hills (whose very name is evocative of Granada and Islamic Spain), but when I drove along the 118 Freeway, I didn't see anything that looked like a mosque. It was only when I was taken there by a friend for Friday afternoon prayer that I realized why I had missed the mosque when I drove past it. From the street, it looked like a school.

I learned that there had been local opposition to the construction of the Islamic Center of Granada Hills. When it was finally built, it was not allowed to look like a "traditional" mosque with a dome and/or minarets, due to neighborhood opposition. In an August 2000 article on this mosque in the *Los Angeles Times*, Margaret Ramirez wrote,

> A building permit was granted, but with 44 restrictions, the most conditions ever placed on a house of worship in the San Fernando Valley. In addition to the neighborhood concerns about traffic and parking, city officials pressured the Islamic Center to build the mosque without the traditional Islamic dome and insisted on a Spanish-style structure to fit the Granada Hills neighborhood. That design was publicly lamented by then-mayor Tom Bradley, who accused the City Council of religious intolerance.

It is ironic to think that a mosque, in a city named for one of the centers of Islamic Spain, was not allowed to look like a Spanish-style mosque. Tragically, this mosque is only blocks away from the North Valley Jewish Community Center, which in August of 1999 was the location of a widely publicized hate-crime shooting. There a White supremacist killed one person, injured five others, and forced the evacuation of children and staff from the Jewish day school at the community center.

There are also major Shi'a centers in the United States, such as the Al-Khoei Mosque described above in Queens. Also in Southern California, we have the Islamic Educational Center of Orange County (IECOC) in Costa Mesa, across from the John Wayne Airport. (There's a line here waiting to be made about American Muslims being as American as, well, John Wayne.) The IECOC was started in 1996, and in 1999 was able to move to its current location. It is a mosque that welcomes all Muslims, and as a Sunni Muslim, I have been fortunate to pray there a few times. The imam of the mosque is Sayed Moustafa Al-Qazwini, whose younger brother, Sayed Hassan Al-Qazwini, was the imam of the Islamic Center of America in Dearborn. It was at the Islamic Center of America that the U.S. Postal Service unveiled the latest iteration of the Eid postage stamp on June 10, 2016.

Hassan Al-Qazwini had left his position in Dearborn a year earlier, in a dispute over allocation of funds to a charity in Iraq. For Imam Al-Qazwini, the dispute was more about Iraqi versus Lebanese members of his community. So American Muslims are no strangers to the tensions that sometimes take place among religious leaders in America and their congregations over the issue of funds and which ethnic community benefits from them.

Dearborn is well known to people as having the largest concentration of Muslims in the United States. One often hears ludicrous statements about Dearborn, such as that Shari'a law is in effect, or that non-Muslims are not allowed in the city (the so-called "no-go zone"). This comes as a surprise to the mayor of the city, Jack O'Reilly, who is a Christian. But it is interesting to reflect on the fact that the headquarters of the Ford Motor Company, one of the companies that helped to make American business great, is in a city that now has a large Muslim population. (And, full disclosure, my father spent over thirty years working at the Ford plant in Oakville, Ontario. I spent summers in university building F-series pickups alongside my father, so I have a special connection to Ford.)

In 2015 the Women's Mosque of America was opened in Los Angeles. It was founded by M. Hasna Masnavi, a filmmaker and comedy writer who has long been involved with Muslim communities in that city. It is the first women's only mosque in the United States, and as such attracted a lot of media attention when it opened. The Friday prayers are held in the Pico Union Project, which was built in 1909 as the home of Sinai Temple, and which is the oldest synagogue building in Los Angeles. The building was refurbished in 2012 and provides a splendid example of interfaith cooperation between Jews and Muslims. The mosque allows American Muslim women to develop their own leadership roles within the American Muslim community.

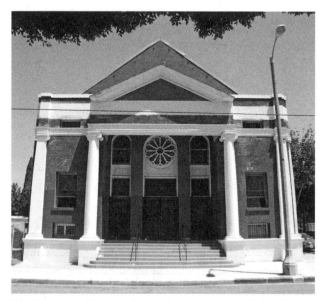

The Women's Mosque of America, at the Pico Union Project

ISLAM IN AMERICAN ARCHITECTURE

In President Obama's 2009 talk, he spoke about how American Muslims have "built our tallest building." He was talking about a Muslim engineer from Bangladesh, Fazlur Rahman Khan, who helped to redefine the American skyline. Khan came to America in 1952 on a Fulbright grant. He studied engineering at the University of Illinois at Urbana-Champaign, where Gulzar Haider would come a decade later.

Khan did his MA and PhD in structural engineering at Urbana-Champaign, and began to work for Skidmore, Owings and Merrill in Chicago, one of the largest architectural firms in the world. He helped to design the U.S. Air Force Academy in Colorado Springs, Colorado. Fifteen years after arriving in the United States, Khan became an American citizen. He came up with the tube frame system that allowed for the construction of unusually tall buildings. He did this first with an apartment building in 1963, the DeWitt-Chestnut Apartments in Chicago. Khan used a modification of an X-brace to his tube frame design when he worked on the John Hancock Center a few years later. His tubular design was used to build the World Trade Center, at the time the tallest building in the United States. It was foreign Muslims, nineteen hijackers, who took down those buildings. But it was an American Muslim, Fazlur Rahman Khan, who made those magnificent buildings possible in the first place.

In 1971, when Khan received an award as "engineering man of the year," he made the following statement: "The technical man must not be lost in his own technology. He must be able to appreciate life; and life is art, drama, music, and most importantly, people." That quote is now part of the memorial plaque to him on the Onterie Center in Chicago, whose brace structure is dedicated to Khan.

In 1973 he used another version of his tube frame, the bundled tube, in his design for the Sears (now Willis) Tower. That was the tallest building in the world for quite some time, and the tallest building in the United States until the opening of One World Trade Center in 2014. So for some forty years, an American Muslim was responsible for the tallest building in America. Think for a minute only about the Chicago skyline. With all of its architectural jewels, we can't imagine that skyline without either the Sears Tower or the John Hancock Center. And we couldn't imagine those buildings without an American Muslim engineer who made them possible. Khan lived out the best American ideals of creating inventions to benefit the world.

ISLAM IN AMERICAN CULTURE

Just as Muslims have helped literally to build America, we have made contributions to American culture. At the beginning of the twentieth century, the poet who was selling the most in America was reported to have been Jalal al-Din Rumi, a Muslim mystic who was born in Afghanistan, died in what is now Turkey, wrote in both Persian and Arabic, and had been dead for over seven hundred years. Some of this popularity came through the translations of Coleman Barks, who could make Rumi's poetry speak to modern Americans. Others came to treasure Rumi from the scholarly translations of people like William C. Chittick, who could accurately translate not just Rumi's Persian or Arabic texts, but the deeply Islamic themes, rooted in the Qur'an and the traditions of the Prophet, that suffuse Rumi's poetry.

In 1979 the Dar al Islam ("House of Islam") community was established in Abiquiu, New Mexico. This was the first planned Muslim community in the United States. The buildings, including a beautiful adobe mosque and school, were designed by Egyptian architect Hassan Fathy and opened in 1982. The community never became the permanent settlement envisioned by its founders, but it has continued as an Islamic educational and retreat center.

There has been an American fascination with Sufism, the mystical tradition of Islam, since at least the work of Alexander Russell Webb, who in 1893 made connections between Theosophy and Islam. Marcia Hermansen has documented the numerous Sufi groups in the United States. While membership in these various Sufi communities is small compared to the number of Muslims in the United States, one sees their impact in popular culture, like the popularity of Rumi's poetry. Starting in the 1980s, I saw a growth in the religion bookshelves of most major bookstores to include a section on Sufism. Often, there were more books on Sufism than on Islam. Zain Abdullah has documented some of the public performances of Sufis in America. This has taken place in New York City for some thirty years, among West African Muslims of the Murid Sufi order. This is the annual Cheikh Amadou Bamba Day parade on July 28. The parade begins on 7th Avenue and winds its way to 125th Street and the "Little Touba" neighborhood where many of the participants live. It's a stunning sight, to see them marching next to the Masjid Malcolm Shabazz, and think of the connections to the African American Muslim who was one of the key figures in the civil rights movement.

American Muslims have begun to influence American higher education. One may be aware of this in the sciences and engineering, where a number of Muslims have taught with distinction. Most notably, and referenced in President Obama's 2009 speech, in 1999 Ahmed Zewail, who teaches at the California Institute of Technology, won a Nobel Prize in chemistry. This was some seventeen years after he became an American citizen. American Muslim academics have also influenced the humanities and liberal arts, especially in the study of Islam.

I began going to the annual meetings of the American Academy of Religion (AAR) in 1992. The AAR is the largest scholarly group in the United States for the study of religion. The Study of Islam section of the AAR had been organized only a few years before, in 1986, arising out of an earlier Islamic Studies group. At that time, I would estimate that there were no more than seventy-five of us who specialized in the study of Islam, with only a few of us being Muslim. A decade later, the listserv for the group had expanded to some two hundred scholars. Now, there are over eight hundred people who subscribe to that academic list. There are more panels than ever about Islam at the AAR, and some four hundred to five hundred scholars of Islam who participate at the annual meeting. In addition to the Study of Islam section, there is the contemporary Islam group; the Islam, gender, and women group; the Islamic mysticism group; and the Qur'an group. I would estimate that at least a quarter to perhaps a third of those five hundred scholars of Islam are now Muslim scholars of Islam. That changes the dynamic, as we all know. It's one thing, for example, to have a conversation about African Americans. It's a very different conversation, however, if African Americans are part of it.

One sees that connection to African Americans with the linking of Martin Luther King Jr. and Malcolm X, the link that James Cone has described between Islam and

Black theology. Islam often was an alternative to "White" or "Western" in African American movements. Here, for example, I think of the work of Cheryl Clarke from *"After Mecca": Women Poets and the Black Arts Movement*:

> The use of the trope "Mecca" resonates with black consciousness movements of the 1960s and 1970s in the United States, a demand to turn away from the (white) West. . . . "Mecca," then, comes to represent the struggle of black people, during the late twentieth century, to envision a world in which African American culture occupied the center. This "Mecca" is as much to be struggled toward as struggled for—much like Malcolm X's "hadj" and Martin Luther King's "mountaintop," one is always getting there. (2)

In 1998 comedian Dave Chappelle converted to Islam. At that time, he wasn't famous, with a few minor film roles to his credit. That same year, he had his biggest hit to date, the cult film *Half-Baked*, which he cowrote and starred in. Any film labeled a "cult" film obviously doesn't have blockbuster status, but it also introduced a number of young people to the young comedian. Chappelle did his first HBO comedy special in 2000, and from 2003 to 2006 was responsible for one of the funniest shows ever on American television, the groundbreaking *Chappelle's Show*. None of the characters in the show were Muslim, but he featured Muslim Hip Hop artists such as Mos Def and Talib Kweli among his first musical guests. I don't think I heard Chappelle talk publicly about being a Muslim until an interview in *Time* magazine in 2005 and then the following year on *Inside the Actor's Studio* with James Lipton.

Every artist that I know wants to be recognized first and foremost as an artist, not as a member of an ethnic or linguistic or religious group. Dave Chappelle represents something important here. He became famous because he was a fabulous writer and stand-up comedian, not because he was a Muslim. He never expressed any kind of "Muslim identity" on *Chappelle's Show*, which I would argue was one of the most important American cultural products (not just television shows) of the first decade of the twenty-first century. Yet there he was, an American Muslim who like others before him influenced American culture, another outstanding American cultural producer.

One sees this influence in unlikely places. For example, one often doesn't think first of Latinos/Latinas when the subject of American Muslims arises. Yet Latina/o Muslims are an important part of the fabric of American Muslim life. To mention only one city, Los Angeles is home to the Los Angeles Latino Muslim Association. One finds similar groups in other American cities with large Latina/o populations. My friend César Domínguez is one of the most important Muslim leaders in Los Angeles, and he happens to be of Mexican descent. For many Latinos/Latinas, there is a connection to Islam because of the roots that Spanish shares with Arabic, an intertwining of Muslim and Catholic cultures in Islamic Spain. There is also a shared devotion to Mary, the mother of Jesus.

A different kind of connection occurred as a result of the terrorist attacks of 9/11. One of the first calls I got in the aftermath of 9/11 was from the pastor of a Japanese American Methodist Church, Rev. Ruy Mizuki. Comparisons were already being made between 9/11 and the attack on Pearl Harbor, and Rev. Mizuki knew that this road led to internment. When we interned Japanese Americans after the attack on Pearl Harbor, even though we knew they were loyal Americans, very few other Americans spoke out in their defense. Rev. Mizuki wanted to speak out, as a Japanese American, for Muslim Americans. This began a friendship between Japanese Americans and Muslim Americans that has continued to this day. Muslim Americans join Japanese Americans, for example, on the annual pilgrimage to Manzanar, one of the internment camps in the Owens Valley of California.

ISLAMIC ART

American Muslims have influenced Islamic art, not just in America, but around the world. Mohamed Zakariya is one of the finest calligraphers in the Islamic world, and the best Islamic calligrapher in the United States. He is credited with starting Islamic calligraphy in the United States. Born in Ventura, California in 1942, he moved with his family to Los Angeles. While walking along Wilshire Boulevard as a boy, he saw his first example of Islamic calligraphy in the window of an Armenian carpet store. Zakariya eventually dropped out of high school and worked for a time in a machine shop. Having saved enough money, he took a trip to Morocco in his late teens, a time in which many Americans were going to India and "the mystic east." There, he became fascinated with Islam and Islamic calligraphy. On his return to the United States, he converted to Islam.

He returned on other journeys to North Africa and the Middle East, and spent some time studying manuscripts in the British Museum in London. Studying first with the Egyptian calligrapher Abdussalam Ali-Nour, Zakariya in 1984 became a student of the Turkish master calligrapher, Hasan Celebi. In 1988 Zakariya received his diploma from Celebi at the Research Center for Islamic History, Art and Culture in Istanbul, the first American to achieve this honor. He received his second diploma, in the *ta'lik* script, from Ali Alparslan in 1997.

Zakariya lives with his family in Arlington, Virginia. His work has been displayed in various museums and galleries, and is in a number of private collections. He wrote the brochure *Music for the Eyes: An Introduction to Islamic and Ottoman Calligraphy* for an exhibit organized by the Los Angeles County Museum of Art and the Metropolitan Museum of Art, which toured America from 1998 to 2000. He was the artist commissioned by the U.S. Postal Service to design their Eid (an Islamic religious festival) stamp, which debuted on September 1, 2001. That stamp has been reissued several times in different designs, with the latest version released on June 10, 2016.

Zakariya recently designed and produced, with his colleague Aasil Ahmed, the Muslim prayer room for Georgetown University, called "The Mosque of the Two Columns." It is a new approach to making a mosque, a high-end result achieved through modest means. It is aimed at realizing deeper worship by providing a more intimate, colorful, and artistic setting.

Zakariya is engaged with teaching calligraphy according to the Ottoman method, producing new work and exhibiting it around the country. He writes contemporary instructional material (available from his website) and translates classic texts to provide deeper knowledge about Islamic calligraphy.

Mohamed Zakariya's work shows that American Islam has become an integral part of the culture of the Muslim world. Instead of American Muslims going to the Islamic world (as Zakariya himself did) to study calligraphy, students from the Muslim world come to the United States to study with an American master.

It is not just American Muslims who are producing American Muslim art. Sandow Birk is a surfer who has

Mohamed Zakariya, Red Hilye, *2010*

traveled extensively around the world searching for waves. Over the past two decades, those travels have taken him on extended trips to various regions of the Islamic world, visiting several of the most populous Muslim nations and seeing important collections of Islamic artworks. It was these travels, along with political events across the world, that inspired his initial interest in Islam and the Qur'an. Since beginning the project, he has continued his travels to a variety of places, from the largest mosque in Africa to the remote Islamic outposts of Mindanao in the Philippines and the Andaman Islands of India. He has done research throughout Morocco; at the Institut du Monde Arab in Paris while on a three-month residency at the Cité International des Artes; and at the Chester Beatty Library in Dublin, home to one of the largest and finest collections of hand-illuminated Qur'ans in the world. Further research was done at the Smithsonian's Freer and Sackler Galleries, and the Museu Calouste Gulbenkian in Lisbon.

In his American Qur'an project, Sandow Birk spent the past decade working to create a personal Qur'an. Following the traditions of classical Islamic manuscripts—such as the colors of inks, the formatting of pages, the size of margins, and the illuminations of page headings and medallions marking verses and passages—he has hand-transcribed the entire English-translated text of the Qur'an. His hand-lettered calligraphy uses an American tradition of writing—that of the street letters of urban graffiti that he finds around his Long Beach neighborhood. Once each chapter is transcribed, he then seeks to illuminate the text and its message with scenes from contemporary American life—investigating how the message relates to our lives in the United States today. Adapting the techniques and stylistic devices of Arabic and Persian painting and albums, his works blend the past with the present, the East with the West, creating an American Qur'an. The project was completed in 2015 and published as *American Qur'an* by Norton in 2016.

I first saw part of the project in 2009 at the Koplin del Rio Gallery in Culver City. I admired what Birk was doing, and thought it was a perfect fit of traditional Islamic and contemporary American styles. A few years later, I was able to purchase one of my favorite pieces from this series, his illustration of chapter 55, the chapter known as *Sura Al-Rahman* or the chapter of the Merciful (his translation is "the Beneficent"). The chapter has long been a favorite of mine, with its repeated refrain of "which of the favors of your Lord will you deny?" reminding human beings of the many ways in which God has been merciful to us. I also appreciated the imagery in the painting, of ship-workers doing maintenance work on ships in dry dock. I live in the Marina del Rey area of Los Angeles, and come from a working class background in which my father was a mechanic, so the piece has a double resonance of home for me.

And the United States has extraordinary collections of Islamic art. The Los Angeles County Museum of Art (LACMA), to take my hometown example, has one of the finest collections of Islamic art in the world, at over 1,700 pieces. There are also important collections at the Smithsonian Museum in Washington, D.C., and at the Metropolitan Museum of Art in New York City. Another spectacular collection is that of the Doris Duke Foundation for Islamic Art, housed in Shangri La, Duke's home in Honolulu. Since

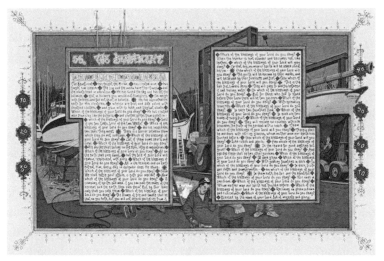

Sandow Birk Illustration of Sura 55

2007, the foundation has sponsored the Building Bridges Program, which as the name implies seeks to build bridges between Muslim and non-Muslim communities.

POLITICS

American Muslims have also played a role in American politics. In 2006 Keith Ellison of Minnesota became the first Muslim elected to Congress. In 2008 André Carson from Indiana became the second Muslim elected to Congress. Both are also African American. A decade earlier, in 1988, the Muslim Public Affairs Council (MPAC) was founded in Los Angeles. MPAC originated from a political action committee of the Islamic Center of Southern California. MPAC is the largest and most important Muslim political group in the United States. But there are lots of Muslims involved in political activity. In New York, for example, one thinks of Linda Sarsour, the executive director of the Arab American Association of New York. She is also the cofounder of MPOWER Change, a grassroots digital Muslim group for progressive causes.

In 2013 the city of Hamtramck, Michigan, became the first Muslim-majority city in the United States. Two years later, it became the first city to elect a city council with a majority of Muslims. This has led to the same negative publicity that neighboring Dearborn has received. The reality, however, is quite different. André Carson, for example, has spoken about his converting to Islam precisely because he saw Muslims in Indianapolis fighting against crime. There is a history here among African Americans that goes back to Malcolm X, who spoke often about how when he was a Christian, he was a criminal, but when he converted to Islam, he straightened out his life. That sometimes is painful for Christians to hear.

American Muslims, as I have highlighted here, have undeniably contributed to American culture. These contributions range from the overt, such as the building of iconic American skyscrapers, to the less visible, such as providing healthcare or educating children. We are engaged, like other Americans, in politics, and in grassroots actions. We, too, are America.

Conclusion
The Poetry of Ordinary American Muslim Lives

"SING ME BACK HOME": MERLE HAGGARD AND
AMERICAN MUSLIMS

On April 6, 2016, we lost one of the great men of twentieth-century American music, Merle Haggard. The Hag, as he was known, was born in Oildale, California, a few miles north of Bakersfield. I was a fan of his music, but when I moved to California State University, Northridge, I got to know something of the man himself through Alyce Akers, who was chair of family and consumer sciences. She was also born in Oildale, a decade or so after Haggard, also of parents that had migrated from Oklahoma. She told me stories of living a mile away from him, and seeing both him and Buck Owens perform at the Blackboard, a rough and tumble joint. Haggard lived in a boxcar that his father had converted into a home. After his father's death when Hag was a boy, he spent his youth as a petty criminal, but also as a musician. He was an inmate in San Quentin when Johnny Cash played and recorded there in 1958, was released in 1960, and pardoned by Governor Ronald Reagan in 1972. The Hag wrote some of the most important songs in country music ("Mama Tried," "Sing Me Back Home," and "Hungry Eyes," to take only a few examples), as well as some of the most execrable ("Okie from Muskogee"). He went through periods of being an outlaw and periods of being a hero. He married Bonnie, the ex-wife of Buck Owens, the other man credited with creating the "Bakersfield sound." It was the "twang" of that Bakersfield sound that cut through the smooth softness of his voice, part of why his music was so appealing. Haggard received a Kennedy Center Honor six years before his death. Merle Haggard, too, is America.

Merle Haggard wasn't the greatest country songwriter ever. That title belongs, with no dispute, and a line drawn under it before mention of anyone else, to Hank Williams Sr. Merle Haggard wasn't the greatest country songwriter of his generation; that would be Kris Kristofferson. Merle Haggard wasn't the American conscience and icon that was Johnny Cash (among my particular group of Cash devotees, it's not that Johnny Cash speaks with the voice of God, it's that God speaks in the voice of Johnny Cash). Merle Haggard wasn't the greatest of the outlaw singer-songwriters; that would be Willie Nelson. But Merle Haggard *was* crucial to understanding American music in the twentieth century. We cannot, to put it simply, imagine or understand American music without his contributions. In that sense, American Muslims *are* Merle Haggard, part of the fabric of American life. You may not think about us, and you may not like us. You may not listen to us. You may go through periods during which you distrust or even despise us. We might live in a major metropolitan center, or perhaps in a relatively "unimportant" part of the country. We may be wealthy, but we also may, as I do, come from humble, working class roots. We aren't the most important or influential group in America's history, but it would be a very different and poorer country without us.

American Muslims have literally helped to build this country. Think of the Muslim slaves like Estevancio who helped to chart this country, who died eighty years before the Pilgrims landed here. Think of the slave labor, including the Muslim slave labor, that helped to build colonial America. The labor that helped to rebuild the White House and other buildings in D.C. that were burned after the War of 1812. That helped to build up Lower Manhattan and, later in the same space, to create Little Syria. That helped to design major skyscrapers that are emblematic of the American skyline.

When I was last in Annapolis, to give a talk at the U.S. Naval Academy, I stayed at the Governor Calvert House, which is across the street from the Maryland State House. The Calvert House dates back to 1695, and when I was there they had a display of artifacts found during the renovations of the property. One of them was a "hand of Fatima," which would have been worn by a female African Muslim slave. When one remembers the slave ships that docked a few blocks away in the Annapolis harbor, this discovery is not surprising. Muslims, it is worth repeating, have been in this country for centuries.

We were brought here, some of us, against our will as slaves. But we were not only slaves. Some of us came here willingly, seeking a new life, just like countless other Americans. We came here—in fact, some of us were recruited and brought here—to work in the textile mills in Maine, and the automotive plants in Michigan. In keeping with American ideals, we were vendors and small business owners, not just in the Midwest, but as far west as Wyoming. Kathryn Schulz did a great portrayal in June 2016 in the *New Yorker* of Zarif Khan, known as Hot Tamale Louie. He was an Afghani Muslim who became a U.S. citizen in 1926, only to have that citizenship stripped at the end of that year because as an Afghan he was not White. He had to wait almost thirty years, until 1954, before he could become a U.S. citizen a second time. He, and other Afghani tamale vendors, made that food popular in the West at the beginning of the twentieth century. Of Khan and his generation, Schulz wrote,

> The history of immigrants is, to a huge extent, the history of this nation, though so is the pernicious practice of determining that some among us do not deserve full humanity, and full citizenship. Zarif Khan was deemed insufficiently American on the basis of skin color; ninety years later, when the presence of Muslims among us had come to seem like a crisis, his descendants were deemed insufficiently American on the basis of faith.

Muslims, we often need to be reminded, are part of the history of America.

"SING ME BACK HOME": MUHAMMAD ALI AND AMERICAN MUSLIMS

On June 3, 2016, we lost the Greatest of All Time, Muhammad Ali. I was in Ottawa, Canada, that week, visiting with some friends, including one who is a member of the Canadian Parliament. I woke up on the morning of Saturday, June 4, in the home of my friends Derek Evans and Pat Deacon to hear the news of Ali's death. Derek is a Canadian writer, consultant, and former deputy secretary of Amnesty International. He told me that he had been listening for the past several hours to the early morning radio coverage on the BBC, which had solely been reporting on Ali's death. In the airports that day in Ottawa and Toronto, heading back home to Los Angeles, the television stations were all tuned to coverage of his death, indicating the global concern. It wasn't just Americans who cared that the Greatest was gone, but Canadians and Brits and in fact the whole world. An American Muslim, we need to remind ourselves, was the most famous man in the world.

Ali indeed "shook up the world," not just with the brilliance of his athleticism, but with the beauty of his spirit. He refused induction into the Vietnam War because of his religious beliefs as a Muslim, at a time in which people in the United States still supported that war. Two years after Ali's refusal, for example, Merle Haggard released "Okie from Muskogee," with its line about not burning one's draft card. The single went to number one on the country charts, and was voted the country single and record of the year by the Country Music Association in 1970. The Hag reflected the temper of his times, but Ali won the day when Americans turned against the war.

Muhammad Ali spoke out continuously as an American Muslim. His voice grew softer as he aged, and he no longer spoke in the brash and loud voice of his youth. We might not have heard him, we might not have listened, but that soft voice was still speaking. One of his last public statements was to NBC News on December 9, 2015:

> I am a Muslim and there is nothing Islamic about killing innocent people in Paris, San Bernardino, or anywhere else in the world. True Muslims know that the ruthless violence of so called Islamic Jihadists goes against the very tenets of our religion.

> We as Muslims have to stand up to those who use Islam to advance their own personal agenda. They have alienated many from learning about Islam. True Muslims know or should know that it goes against our religion to try and force Islam on anybody.

> Speaking as someone who has never been accused of polit-
> ical correctness, I believe that our political leaders should
> use their position to bring understanding about the religion
> of Islam and clarify that these misguided murderers have
> perverted people's views on what Islam really is.

While Ali didn't name any political leader in question, his statement was titled "Presidential Candidates Proposing to Ban Muslim Immigration to the United States." In the end, Ali was classy, which couldn't be said about the politician to whom he was referring (and who often used that word, "classy," for himself). Ali's public funeral was held during the first week of Ramadan, on June 10, 2016, in his hometown of Louisville, Kentucky. The funeral was by design an interfaith event, featuring remarks by religious leaders, family members, celebrities, and politicians, concluding with a eulogy from former president Bill Clinton. The service was arranged by my friend Timothy Gianotti, who was the religious advisor to Muhammad Ali and his family. I first met Timothy when we were both graduate students at the University of Toronto, and it was lovely to see the service that he had coordinated after years of working on it with Ali and his family. The service began with a procession through the streets of his hometown that ended with his Muslim burial in the Cave Hill Cemetery. However, the day before, Ali had also had a traditional Muslim funeral service, or *janazah*. At his passing, his body was washed and shrouded in accordance with Islamic customs. Muslims across America and around the world were encouraged to hold *janazah* prayers for our deceased Muslim brother.

The *janazah* prayer for Ali was extraordinary, held on June 9, 2016, at the Kentucky Exposition Center in Louisville. This was next to Freedom Hall, where Ali had fought Tunney Hunsaker in his first professional fight on

October 29, 1960. I watched the funeral service online, as many people did, in my case on a YouTube feed from Fox 10 News, the Fox-owned and -operated television station in Phoenix, Arizona. The irony was rich. Here was a television station, Fox, not noted for its sympathetic coverage of Muslims, covering live the full Islamic prayer service for Muhammad Ali. On the drive home, I heard part of the Qur'an recitation from the funeral on CBS radio, the first time I ever heard coverage of a Muslim funeral on the recap of the daily news.

The service was led by Imam Zaid Shakir, a noted American imam from California and the cofounder of Zaytuna College, the first accredited Muslim liberal arts college in the United States. The coffin was brought in by pallbearers that included Shaikh Hamza Yusuf (another cofounder of Zaytuna College) and international recording star Yusuf Islam (the former Cat Stevens). Imam Zaid explained to the crowd what would happen, as the *janazah* prayer is unique in that there is no bowing or prostration, only four cycles of prayer during which the congregation remains standing. The funeral prayer was performed, followed by a Qur'an recitation and a translation of the words recited by Shaikh Hamza. Then three people were invited to give short sermons to the crowd. They were Sherman Jackson, a professor at USC and one of the most important Muslim scholars in the United States; Dalia Mogahed, the former director of the Gallup Center for Muslim Studies; and Khadija Sharif-Drinkard, a lawyer who oversees business and legal affairs for the New York offices of Black Entertainment Television (BET). That two of the three were Muslim women (who were also successful businesswomen) was important to show the leadership roles of American Muslim women.

Sherman Jackson is one of the most important American Muslim scholars, a mentor and friend for years. Professor Jackson's short sermon was brilliant, and a few lines from it captured the intertwining of American and Muslim identities in the body of Muhammad Ali:

> As a cultural icon, Ali made being Muslim cool. Ali made being a Muslim dignified. Ali made being a Muslim relevant. And all of this he did in a way that no one could challenge his belongingness to or in this country. Ali put the question of whether a person can be a Muslim and an American to rest. Indeed, he KO'd that question. With his passing, let us hope that that question will now be interred with his precious remains . . . Ali helped this country move closer to its own ideals. He helped America do and see some things that America was not quite ready to do or see on its own. And because of Ali's heroic efforts, America is a better place today for us all. And in this regard, Ali belongs not just to the Muslims of this country, Ali belongs to all Americans. . . . If you are an American, Ali is part of your history, part of what makes you who you are, and as an American, Ali belongs to you, and you too should be proud of this precious piece of your American heritage.

At another funeral service over fifty years earlier, on February 27, 1965, Ossie Davis gave the eulogy for Malcolm X. There, he famously said, "Malcolm was our manhood, our living, black manhood! This was his meaning to his people. And in honoring him we honor the best in ourselves." Ali, as Professor Jackson pointed out, wasn't just for *his* people, but for all people. If Malcolm was our manhood, then Ali was our humanity, with a life lived for all the world to see. A life lived in complexity and contradiction, triumph and tragedy. A life, as Gary Smith reminded us in the introduction to this book, of change and metamorphosis. An iconic American life, lived by an iconic American Muslim.

So let us sing Ali back home as the American Muslim hero that he was, and in the words of Merle Haggard's song, "make [our] old memories come alive." Remember the tributes across America and around the world to this American Muslim. Muhammad Ali, too, an American Muslim, *is* America.

And when we sing, let us remember another American Muslim who made possible so many of the songs discussed in the second chapter, Ahmet Ertegun, the cofounder of Atlantic Records. Simply put, he changed the face of music. Not just American music, but popular music around the world in the twentieth century. And Ahmet Ertegun did this as an American Muslim. An immigrant who in the classic American parable came here as a boy with his family, and made a new life for himself. In the process, he helped to enrich the music of all of our lives.

THE POETRY OF ORDINARY MUSLIM LIVES

Muhammad Ali and Ahmet Ertegun were, of course, extraordinary. We will not see their like again. But there are millions of ordinary Muslims living out their lives in America. Those lives give the lie to the popular prejudices that surround them: that they are violent, that they are misogynist, that they have not denounced terrorism and violence, and that they are a threat to our American way of life. Instead, the reality is that American Muslims represent the American way of life. In this regard, we are very different from European or Canadian Muslim communities.

Canadian Muslims do not have the same history that American Muslims do. The first census in Canada, in 1871 (the modern country came into existence in 1867), listed thirteen Muslims. So there was a small Muslim population in Canada at the end of the nineteenth century, but it was nothing like the number of Muslim slaves that were present in America generations earlier. There is no comparable component in Canadian Muslim life that resembles African American Muslims, who represent at least one-quarter of American Muslims. African American Muslims, as Americans, have for centuries been part of the history of the United States.

In Europe the situation is markedly different, both among the Muslim and non-Muslim populations, which each tend to be much more homogeneous than they are in the United States. So in Britain, the majority of Muslims have their origins in South Asia. In France, Muslims are mostly from North Africa. In Germany, Muslims are usually Turks or Kurds. Contrast that with the American situation, where Muslims are equally African American, South Asian, or Middle Eastern (to take only the three largest groups). Also, there are narrower definitions of what it means to be French or English or German than of what it means to be American, which incorporates all of those European identities and many others.

There is also a socioeconomic difference. American Muslims are an American success story, solidly middle class and mostly professional. There are thousands of American Muslim physicians, for example, perhaps as many as twenty thousand if one looks at information from the Islamic Medical Association of North America. European Muslims by contrast are marginalized, often in a much lower socioeconomic class with much higher rates of unemployment. Sometimes, as is often the case in Germany, they are in the status of migrants or guest workers, not citizens.

Finally, there is a difference between American-style secularism—which doesn't seek to abolish religion but rather to give all religions an equal seat at the table—and the European disestablishment of religion, which seeks to make the public space nonreligious. In the United States, American Muslims are free to live out their Islam in the public space. And there are so many American Muslims who do this, of whom so many Americans aren't aware. One thinks for example of Tayyibah Taylor, who died on September 4, 2014. Taylor was an American Muslim woman who in 2000 cofounded *Azizah Magazine* in Atlanta, a magazine for and by American Muslim women. Volume 8, issue 2 of the magazine was titled "Remembering Trailblazers" and featured stories on the life and work of five extraordinary American Muslim women: Tayyibah Taylor, Sharifa Alkhateeb, Aliyah Abdul-Karim, Maryam Ali, and Mufeedah Abdul-Karim. None of them are household names in America, but all made significant contributions to the life and work of American Muslim women.

Another example is the UMMA Clinic, which for twenty years has been providing free health care to people in need. *Umma* is the Arabic word for community, used by Muslims to refer to the believing community of Muslims, in the same way that Christians use the word "church." However, in this case, it is an acronym that stands for the University Muslim Medical Association. The UMMA Clinic was founded in 1992 when Muslim students at UCLA wanted to provide health care to people in need, as both their duty as good citizens and as good Muslims. They worked with the various agencies in Los Angeles and in 1996 opened a clinic on Florence Avenue in South Los Angeles, which is classified federally as a "medically underserved area." By that time, some of those students had become physicians. Most of the patients who are seen and served at the clinic are Latino/a or African American Christians, so this isn't

Muslim physicians helping out other Muslims, but Muslims helping out other Americans. And isn't that one of our highest ideals, to help out our neighbors who are in need.

In 2013 they partnered with Fremont High School to create the Fremont Wellness Center and Community Garden, which serves both the high school and the surrounding community. This is an opportunity to get health care into a school of over 4,000 students, where one in three are obese, one in thirty will develop type 2 diabetes before leaving the school, and roughly one in seven young women will contract a sexually transmitted disease before the age of twenty. The clinic provides both mental health services and primary care, as well as a community garden to help establish healthy eating habits. It is an outstanding program, but it is not unique, as there are many other free clinics around the country run by Muslim medical professionals.

MUSLIMS IN AMERICA

One often hears talk of "Islam *and* the West" or "Islam *and* America." This brings up an image of two mutually exclusive realities. If we change one simple word, we get instead "Islam *in* the West" or "Islam *in* America." That simple change makes all the difference. Instead of posing two warring factions, "Islam" and "America," we see the reality of their interconnectedness. Islam is, of course, a "Western" religion, sharing deep roots with Judaism and Christianity. Muslims are much closer religiously to Jews and to Christians than we are to "Eastern" religions such as Hinduism and Buddhism. Muslims are also a strong presence in "the West." Islam is the second-largest religion in Canada, Britain, and France, and may well be the second-largest religion in the United States. "Islam in the West" recognizes the entwined heritage of Islam and the West. The West as we know it would not be what it is without the contribution of Muslims. Think quickly of our number system, for example, and ask yourself if it is easier to do multiplication and division with Arabic numbers or with Roman numerals. Yet we don't see our connections, and here in America people often have a fear or hatred of Muslims. In the 2008 presidential campaign, former Secretary of State Colin Powell, a Republican, spoke out against this fear and stereotyping in his own party. On October 19, 2008, on *Meet the Press*, General Powell said:

> . . . I'm also troubled by, not what Senator McCain says, but what members of the party say. And it is permitted to be said such things as, "Well, you know that Mr. Obama is a Muslim." Well, the correct answer is, he is not a Muslim, he's a Christian. He's always been a Christian. But the really right answer is, what if he is? Is there something wrong with being a Muslim in this country? The answer's no, that's not America. Is there something wrong with some seven-year-old Muslim-American kid believing that he or she could be president? Yet, I have heard senior members of my own party drop the suggestion, "He's a Muslim and he might be associated with terrorists." This is not the way we should be doing it in America.

I feel strongly about this particular point because of a picture I saw in a magazine. It was a photo essay about troops who are serving in Iraq and Afghanistan. And one picture at the tail end of this photo essay was of a mother in Arlington Cemetery, and she had her head on the headstone of her son's grave. And as the picture focused in, you could see the writing on the headstone. And it gave his awards—Purple Heart, Bronze Star—showed that he died in Iraq, gave his date of birth, date of death. He was 20 years old. And then, at the very top of the headstone, it didn't have a Christian cross, it didn't have the Star of David, it had a crescent and a

Kareem Rashad Sultan Khan's Headstone,
Arlington National Cemetery

star of the Islamic faith. And his name was Kareem Rashad Sultan Khan, and he was an American. He was born in New Jersey. He was 14 years old at the time of 9/11, and he waited until he can go serve his country, and he gave his life. Now, we have got to stop polarizing ourselves in this way.

American Muslims have served in our military since the Revolutionary War. There were some three hundred Muslim soldiers who served during our Civil War. That's not a large number, certainly, but it also gives the lie to the oft-repeated claim that Muslims are newcomers to this country. We were here before this country was founded, we fought against the British, and we fought in the war that defined who and what we were as a country. At the end of 2015, ABC News reported figures from the U.S. Department of Defense that some 5,896 Muslims were serving in the military. That number may be higher, since some 400,000 service members did not self-identify their faith. So almost 6,000 American Muslims serve in our armed forces, helping to defend our country.

VIOLENCE AND TERRORISM

Since the terrorist attacks of 9/11, one has heard the refrain that Muslims have not denounced terrorism. We did so that very morning of Tuesday, September 11, 2001, before we even knew the full details of what had happened that morning. Here's a sampling from a few different Muslim organizations:

From the Muslim Public Affairs Council:

In response to the criminal attacks against targets in New York City and Washington, D.C., the Muslim Public Affairs Council issued the following statement:

1. We feel that our country, the United States, is under attack.
2. All Americans should stand together to bring the perpetrators to justice.
3. We warn against any generalizations that will only serve to help the criminals and incriminate the innocent.
4. We offer our resources and resolve to help the victims of these intolerable acts, and we pray to God to protect and bless America.

From the American Muslim Political Coordination Council (AMPCC):

American Muslims utterly condemn what are apparently vicious and cowardly acts of terrorism against innocent civilians. We join with all Americans in calling for the swift apprehension and punishment of the perpetrators. No political cause could ever be assisted by such immoral acts.

From the Council on American Islamic Relations (CAIR):

CAIR is calling on Muslims nationwide to offer whatever assistance they can to help the victims of today's terrorist attacks in New York and Washington, D.C.

Muslims in local communities should take the following IMMEDIATE ACTIONS:

* Muslim medical professionals are asked to go to the scenes of the attacks to offer aid and comfort to the victims.
* Muslim relief agencies should contact their counterparts to offer support in the recovery efforts.
* Individual Muslims should donate blood by contacting the local office of the Red Cross. (Call 1-800-GIVE-LIFE.) They should also send donations to those relief agencies that are on the scene of the attacks.

Such sentiments have been repeated countless times, and yet still many are under the impression that Muslims have not denounced terrorism and violence. The website for *The American Muslim* (originally founded as a print magazine in 1989) has pages and pages that document Muslim rejections of violence and terrorism.

In America we still think of violence as something unique to Muslims, and don't seem to realize the violence around us. Charles Kurzman is a sociologist at the University of North Carolina who studies homegrown Muslim terrorism. The numbers are, unfortunately, greater than zero, where they should be. But they are much lower than many people think. So, for example, in 2015 nineteen people were killed by American Muslims in mass shootings. Fourteen were killed by the shooters in San Bernardino, five by the shooter in Chattanooga. Nineteen Americans shot dead at the hands of American Muslim terrorists are nineteen too many. But that number represents the total for *all* of 2015. By comparison, every day in 2015, twenty-two American veterans killed themselves. Every *day* in 2015, more American servicemen and servicewomen, heroes who protected our country, took their own lives than all of the Americans killed in mass shootings by American Muslims that year. Every day, some eighty Americans are shot to death in gun-related violence. So the number of Americans killed in mass shootings by American Muslims in all of 2015 was fewer than the number of Americans killed in any eight-hour period by guns. But it is easier to think that American Muslims are the problem. The alternative is to remind ourselves of the horrific violence in which we find ourselves as Americans, violence that American Muslims have had a very small role in perpetrating.

We also don't think about the contributions that American Muslims have made to law enforcement. This doesn't just include the thousands of Muslims who are members of law enforcement agencies around the country. Instead I am thinking of groups like the Muslim Community Affairs unit of the Los Angeles County Sheriff's Department, which was established in 2007 to build stronger relationships with Muslims in Los Angeles. My local mosque has hosted officers from law enforcement, the Department of Homeland Security, and the FBI. American Muslims are working with, rather than against, law enforcement agencies to make all

Americans safer. This doesn't mean that there won't be other incidents that will take place at the hands of American Muslim extremists. Unfortunately, no community is immune to violent acts by its members. We are not perfect as American Muslims, but then again no human being is, only God.

AMERICAN MUSLIMS

Exactly one month after the terrorist attacks of 9/11, I was asked by the Rotary Club of Simi Valley, California, to speak to their members about Islam and Muslims in America. Simi Valley is a conservative area, home to the Ronald Reagan Presidential Library and Museum. At my talk were the local business leaders who usually make up Rotary clubs around the country, but also present was the chief of the Simi Valley Police Department, Randy Adams. People there were frightened, as was to be expected in the month after the attacks. But they also wanted to learn about the beliefs and practices of their American Muslim neighbors. I asked Chief Adams how many Muslims were in his cells, how many he had arrested over the year. That broke the ice, as Chief Adams smiled and said he couldn't think of any. That led to a discussion of how the Muslims in the community were largely law abiding, not involved in drug- or gang-related activity.

It was a lovely experience for me. The people I spoke with were mostly White, mostly conservative, and mostly Christian. Yet they weren't prejudiced, and wanted to learn about their Muslim neighbors and how their Islam was different from that of the hijackers. That afternoon filled me with hope, a hope that I still carry. We need to learn about each other, Muslim and non-Muslim alike. American Muslims are a diverse group. Since there is no official state religion in the United States, and certainly no state form of Islam, all varieties of Islam are allowed to flourish. So one sees not just Sunni, Imami Shi'a, and Ismaili groups, but also heterodox groups such as the Ahmadiyya, who are unfortunately persecuted in a Muslim-majority country such as Pakistan. One sees open and affirming Muslim groups across the country who welcome the full participation of LGBTQ people, while in Muslim-majority countries, homosexuality may be a criminal offense. We have Muslims who are liberal and Muslims who are conservative and everything in between.

We do not, it is important to mention, want to impose Shari'a or Islamic law in America. Many of us came here precisely because we value the rule of law, and many of us grew up here admiring the ideals of the American legal system. We want to live out our lives as American Muslims, and we do that with various types and degrees of observance. That's also important to remember, that some of us are observant, some of us are not, and many of us have differences of opinion on what it means to be observant. In this way, we are no different than any other religious group in America.

As a minority group, like other minority groups before us, we may request special accommodation. So long as this is consistent with American law, there should be no problem. However, many people in a majority position aren't aware of the privileges they enjoy. To take one example, a few years ago, my university's law school released a calendar that listed the Jewish and Muslim holidays, but not the Christian holidays. A colleague from my university came to me with the calendar in hand, incensed that Christians were somehow being discriminated against. I smiled as I pointed out to her that the calendar was simply listing the Muslim and Jewish holidays, not closing on them. By contrast, the law school was closed for all the Christian holidays, there were no classes on Sunday, and most people know when Christmas occurs. The perception of my friend was that Muslims were getting some sort of special treatment, when in fact that special treatment was reserved for the dominant group.

And while Muslims do encounter discrimination and mistreatment, our experience pales in comparison to the historic injustices of segregation, the internment of Japanese Americans, or slavery, to take only the first three examples that come to mind. In a strange way, that too gives me hope. Not the fact that we are discriminated against because we are Muslims, which of course is dreadful, but rather the knowledge that America began, as Jim Wallis of Sojourners famously reminded us, with the near-genocide of Native Americans and the enslavement of Africans. Islamophobia, I remind my Muslim friends, isn't the same as slavery or Jim Crow laws. Perhaps it is simply our turn to pay our dues so that we can be fully recognized as the Americans that we are. Or to use a more problematic metaphor, perhaps it's now our turn to be "jumped in."

For those unfamiliar with the horrors of gang life, to be jumped in means to go through a brutal ritual of initiation. One cannot fully join the gang unless one is beaten by the other members to show that one can take the pain and the punishment. Only then is one embraced and given love and full membership in the gang. Perhaps in this metaphor, America is the gang, and it is our turn as Muslims to get jumped in to prove that we belong and can have full membership.

We aren't only now taking our rightful place as Muslim Americans, we've done that for centuries. We've contributed to this country and helped in the creation of what it means to be American. We've worked with other religious and ethnic groups. Here, I think of connections with Jewish Americans. I grew up with Jewish friends and Jewish teachers. I've done almost as much work in Jewish-Muslim dialogue as I have in Christian-Muslim dialogue. I'm not unique in this, by any means. At Ali's funeral, comedian Billy Crystal told a story of how Ali volunteered to help him with a fundraising effort at the Hebrew University of Jerusalem. As Crystal said, there was Ali, "the most famous Muslim man in the world, honoring his Jewish friend." In Los Angeles, to take another example, for the past decade we have had New Ground: A Muslim-Jewish Partnership for Change, which brings together Muslims and Jews to create new relationships among them.

We are interdependent, Muslims and non-Muslims in America, connected to and with each other's lives. American Muslims have confidence in our ability to be both good Muslims and good Americans. We've been doing that for centuries.

Bibliographic Note

The Pew Forum on Religion and Public Life has done a lot of good work on American Muslims. Their report from August 30, 2011, *Muslim Americans: No Signs of Growth in Alienation or Support for Extremism*, is a great place to begin. Their website, www.pewresearch.org, has their most recent work. The finding that only 38 percent of Americans know a Muslim is from the American Trends Panel (wave 4), survey conducted May 30–June 30, 2014. Gary Smith has a couple of collections of his sportswriting, *Beyond the Game: The Collected Sportswriting of Gary Smith*, and *Going Deep: 20 Classic Sports Stories*. There is so much good work on Islam in America that Karen Isaksen Leonard has put together a bibliographic guide to that literature, *Muslims in the United States: The State of Research*. Yvonne Haddad and Jane I. Smith did much of the early scholarly work in edited collections such as *The Muslims of America*, *Muslim Communities in North America*, and *Mission to America*. There are a number of more recent edited collections, such as Edward E. Curtis IV's *The Columbia*

Sourcebook of Muslims in the United States, Manning Marable and Hishaam Aidi's *Black Routes to Islam*, or Juliane Hammer and Omid Safi's *The Cambridge Companion to American Islam*. Kambiz GhaneaBassiri has done excellent historical work in his *A History of Islam in America: From the New World to the New World Order*. The quotation from Thomas Jefferson can be found in a February 6, 1821, extract from Jefferson's draft autobiography, available at the website of the Thomas Jefferson Foundation, www.monticello.org. For a complete transcript of President Obama's remarks at Cairo University in June 2009, see https://www.whitehouse.gov/the-press-office/remarks-president-cairo-university-6-04-09.

CHAPTER 1: ISLAM IN AMERICA

The stories of pre-Columbian contact with Muslims are found in Abdullah Hakim Quick's *Deeper Roots: Muslims in the Americas and the Caribbean from before Columbus to the Present*. María Rosa Menocal tells the story of Luis de Torres in *Shards of Love: Exile and the Origins of the Lyric*. Michael Gomez at NYU has done great work on the early history of African Muslims in the Americas. See especially his *Black Crescent: African Muslims in the Americas*. Richard Brent Turner has written about African Muslim slaves in his *Islam in the African-American Experience*. Allan D. Austin has also done work in this area with *African Muslims in Antebellum America*, as has Sylviane Diouf with her *Servants of Allah: African Muslims Enslaved in the Americas*. Diouf's book also discusses female African slaves. The stories of early Muslims in the Americas are found in Edward E. Curtis IV's edited *Encyclopedia of Muslim-American History*. Curtis has done great work on African American Islam, as well as more generally on American Islamic history. The World Trade Center excavation is described in Andrea Mustain, "Details of 18th-Century 'Ground Zero Ship' Revealed," *Live Science*, October 4, 2010. Denise Spellberg's *Thomas Jefferson's Qur'an: Islam and the Founders* tells the history not just of Mr. Jefferson, but also of the Founding Fathers with respect to Islam. Umar F. Abd-Allah has written the definitive biography of Alexander Webb, the most famous early American convert to Islam: *A Muslim in Victorian America: The Life of Alexander Russell Webb*. *The Autobiography of Malcolm X* and Manning Marable's *Malcolm X: A Life of Reinvention* are required reading about Malcolm X.

CHAPTER 2: BLUES FOR ALLAH

Robert Greenfield has written a biography of Ahmet Ertegun entitled *The Last Sultan: The Life of Ahmet Ertegun*. Mattias Gardell writes about music, especially Hip Hop, in his splendid book about the Nation of Islam, *In the Name of Elijah Muhammad: Louis Farrakhan and the Nation of Islam*. The best work on the Five Percenters is by Michael Muhammad Knight, both his *The Five Percenters: Islam, Hip-hop and the Gods of New York* and *Blue-Eyed Devil*. Felicia M. Miyakawa also writes about the group in her book *Five Percenter Rap: God Hop's Music, Message, and Black Muslim Mission*. Hisham Aidi has written extensively about Islam and music. See his 2011 article for the *Middle East Report*, "The Grand (Hip-Hop) Chessboard: Race, Rap and Raison d'État" and his magisterial book *Rebel Music: Race, Empire, and the New Muslim Youth Culture*. Su'ad Abdul Khabeer has a new book on American Muslim culture, *Muslim Cool: Race, Religion, and Hip Hop in the United States*.

CHAPTER 3: THE GREATEST

Kareem Abdul-Jabbar has written a number of autobiographical books, including *Giant Steps* and *Kareem.* He wrote about the 1968 boycott in a 2008 article in the *Los Angeles Times*, available at http://articles.latimes .com/2008/may/05/sports/sp-kareemchina5. The *Journal of Sport History* has an article by John Smith about Kareem and the 1968 boycott: http://library.la84.org/SportsLibrary/ JSH/JSH2009/JSH3602/jsh3602g.pdf. For Kareem's own thoughts on his conversion, see "Why I Converted to Islam," AlJazeera America, March 29, 2015, http://america .aljazeera.com/opinions/2015/3/why-i-converted-to-islam .html. Zareena Grewal has directed a documentary film on Mahmoud Abdul-Rauf, *By the Dawn's Early Light: Chris Jackson's Journey to Islam.* A video of Muhammad Ali's *janazah* prayer service, including remarks by Sherman Jackson, can be found on Fox 10 Phoenix's YouTube channel at https://www.youtube.com/watch?v=q_3zm3Wuaxk.

CHAPTER 4: MUSLIMS ON THE AMERICAN LANDSCAPE

Barbara Daly Metcalf has edited a great collection about how Muslims have created their own Muslim spaces in *Making Muslim Space in North America and Europe.* Jack Shaheen has written the definitive work on how Hollywood films misrepresent and stereotype both Arabs and Muslims, *Reel Bad Arabs: How Hollywood Vilifies a People.* On Rumi, see the work of William C. Chittick, especially his translations in *The Sufi Path of Love.* Marcia Hermansen has documented American Sufi movements in her article in *The Muslim World*, "Hybrid Identity Formations in Muslim America: The Case of American Sufi Movements." Zain Abdullah has written about African Muslims in New York City in his book *Black Mecca: The African Muslims of*

Harlem, as well as his article in the *Journal of the American Academy of Religion*, "Sufis on Parade: The Performance of Black, African and Muslim Identities." Cheryl Clarke has written about the use of Islamic tropes in African American art and literature in her *"After Mecca": Women Poets and the Black Arts Movement*. Mohamed Zakariya's work can be found on his website, http://mohamedzakariya.com/. For information on mosques in America, see the publications of the Council on American-Islamic Relations, and in particular the two-part "The American Mosque 2011," available at https://www.cair.com/publications/reports -and-surveys.html.

CONCLUSION

Muhammad Ali's statement to NBC News is included in Alex Johnson's article "Muhammad Ali Hits at Trump and 'Misguided Murderers' Sabotaging Islam," December 9, 2015, http://www.nbcnews.com/news/us-news/muham mad-ali-hits-trump-misguided-murderers-sabotaging -islam-n477351. For specific examples of Muslim rejections of violence and terrorism from *The American Muslim*, see http://theamericanmuslim.org/tam.php/tam/categories/ C167. A transcript of Colin Powell's October 19, 2008, *Meet the Press* interview can be found at NBCNews.com, http:// www.nbcnews.com/id/27266223/ns/meet_the_press/t/ meet-press-transcript-oct/.

IMAGE CREDITS

(Chapter 1) Image of Al-Masudi's pre-956 AD map of the world (date unknown), provided by Jim Siebold; photo-graph of eighteenth-century wooden ship at the 9/11 site by Lucas Jackson, Reuters; *Portrait of Yarrow Mamout* by American artist Charles Willson Peale (1741–1827), item

77 in the Bridging Cultures Bookshelf: Muslim Journeys, National Endowment for the Humanities; official presidential portrait of Thomas Jefferson (1800) by American artist Rembrandt Peale (1778–1860), White House Collection/White House Historical Association; title page from Thomas Jefferson's copy of the Qur'an (London: Printed for L. Hawes, W. Clarke, and R. Collins . . . and T. Wilcox . . . , 1764), located at the Library of Congress; photograph of Congressman Ellison's swearing-in ceremony by Michaela McNichol, Library of Congress; photograph of John Paul Jones' tomb by Kevin H. Tierney, U.S. Navy; Tripoli Monument by sculptor Giovanni C. Micali, full-length photograph by DeviantArt/FantasyStock, detail photograph by author; U.S. Supreme Court frieze by sculptor Adolph Weinman, photograph from the Library of Congress. (Chapter 2) Photograph of Ahmet Ertegun with Kid Rock by Clay Patrick McBride, from the CD booklet for *Rock n Roll Jesus* (2007). (Chapter 3) February 4, 1974 *Sports Illustrated* cover photograph of Muhammad Ali by Tony Triolo. (Chapter 4) Shrine Auditorium by architects John C. Austin and Abram M. Edelman, photograph by Bruce Boehner; Camel cigarettes logo designed by Fred Otto Kleesattel, photograph by Baylor University Press; Trump Taj Mahal by architect Francis X. Dumont, photograph by Kevin Wong; photograph of the Pico Union Project, meeting space for the Women's Mosque of America, by Floyd B. Bariscale; photographs of Mohamed Zakariya's *Red Hilye* and Sandow Birk's illustration of sura 55 provided by the artists. (Chapter 5) Photograph of Kareem Rashad Sultan Khan's headstone, Arlington National Cemetery, by M. R. Patterson.